DESTINATION

Easter!

Lenten Programs and Practices for Youth

Kaylea Hutson worked in a youth ministry team at Nicholasville (Kentucky) United Methodist Church while earning a Master of Divinity degree. She learned the true meaning of youth ministry after finding candy stuck to the inside of her car after a retreat and while lodging five teenage girls in her seminary dorm room for an Ichthus weekend sleepover. Now, as children's pastor for Asbury United Methodist Church, Wichita, Kansas, Kaylea designs "ooey gooey games" and *Veggie Tales* lock-ins.

Kathy Hershman serves as Youth and Program Director at Ogden Memorial United Methodist Church in Princeton, Kentucky. Taking her faith into the community, she also works with Habitat for Humanity, the local ministerial association, and the school district's Emergency Crisis Response Team. Kathy also sponsors a Christian Club in the local schools. She lives with her husband, Don, and son, Kyle. She also has two adult daughters and two granddaughters.

DESTINATION EASTER
Lenten Programs and Practices for Youth
by Kathy Hershman and Kaylea Hutson
Cover and book design by Diana Maio
Copyright © 1998 by Abingdon Press
All rights reserved.
ISBN 0-687-06002-8

Scripture quotations in this publication, unless otherwise indicated, are from the *New Revised Standard Version of the Bible*, copyrighted © 1989 by the Division of Christian Education of the National Council of the Churches of Christ in the United States of America, and are used by permission. All rights reserved.

MANUFACTURED IN THE UNITED STATES OF AMERICA

01 02 03 04 05 06 07—10 9 8 7 6 5 4 3 2

Contents

10 QUESTIONS Youth Will Ask

1. What exactly is Lent?

Lent is a time of preparation for Easter, which is the celebration of the Jesus' resurrection. During this season of preparation, some people fast or give up something important to them. Some spend time in study, devotion, and prayer. Others cut back on their social life and give more time to service in the community.

2. What does the word "Lent" mean?

The word *Lent* comes from the Old English word *lencten*, which refers to the lengthening of days and the coming of spring.

3. Where is Lent mentioned in the Bible?

Lent is not specifically mentioned in the Bible, but it is biblical nonetheless! Jewish tradition, based on the laws given in Torah, the first five books of the Old Testament, has always said that for every religious festival, there must be enough time for preparation. This idea carried over, without question, into Christianity.

4. When does Lent begin and end?

Lent lasts 40 days, beginning on Ash Wednesday and ending at sunset on Easter Eve.

5. Where did the number 40 come from?

In early times each number was felt to reveal a certain aspect of God. The early church fathers felt that the number 40, whether it was 40 hours, 40 days, or 40 years, was the necessary period for cleansing, testing, and strengthening. Using the number 40 is based on the following:

† Noah's ark floated in the flood for 40 days (Genesis 7:4).
† Moses fasted 40 days before he received the Ten Commandments (Exodus 24:18).
† The Israelites wandered in the desert for 40 years before entering the Promised Land (Exodus 16:35).
† Jesus fasted 40 days between his baptism and the beginning of his ministry (Matthew 4:2).

✝ The Risen Christ walked with his disciples for 40 days between Easter and Ascension (Acts 1:3).

✝ Also, 40 days is approximately 10 percent of the year. This is why Lent is sometimes called a "tithe of the year."

6. Why do people say that Lent lasts 40 days when it really lasts 46 days?

Sundays are not counted in Lent, since Sundays are always considered to be "little Easters."

7. How long has Lent been observed?

The earliest observances of Lent were in the days of the apostles. At that time, they observed 40 hours between Good Friday and Easter morning to commemorate the Crucifixion and Resurrection. The time was extended to 40 days at the Council of Nicaea in A.D. 325 and has remained unchanged since then.

8. Why don't Lent and Easter fall at the same time every year?

The method of determining the date for Easter has remained unchanged for more than 1,600 years. Easter begins the first Sunday after the full moon crosses the celestial equator, about March 30 of each year. At this time, day and night are of equal length everywhere. Easter will always fall between March 22 and April 25. Once you establish when Easter is, you simply count backward to determine the beginning of Lent.

9. Why do people give up something for Lent?

Many people give up something they enjoy for Lent. For example, many give up a favorite food for all of Lent or fast for certain meals. Others give up a favorite activity, like watching television. Giving up these things we enjoy become love gifts to God, given to God in adoration and praise. Making a sacrifice, even a small one, helps people recall the great sacrifice Christ made for us all.

10. What is Holy Week?

Holy Week commemorates the last week of Jesus' earthly life. It begins on Palm Sunday and culminates with Easter Sunday. (Refer to Holy Week Journey, pages 12–13.)

HOW TO USE
Destination Easter

DESTINATION EASTER has two main sections: programs and practices. Each program (except Easter) has a Practice of Faith that goes along with it. While the programs provide an opportunity to learn by listening, discussing, and studying, the practices of faith provide an opportunity to learn by creative expression and personal experience.

In DESTINATION EASTER, each program and practice of faith can stand on its own. This design leaves your options wide open. Do them all, or do only a few. Choose what will work best for you and your youth. Here are two sample schedules to consider. These will incorporate all or most of both the programs and practices.

1. Let's do it all!

For this option, you can set up a special Lenten study group or use Sunday school time for the programs and youth meeting times for the practice of the faith. Even if you have youth who do not attend the study group or Sunday school, the practice of faith provides adequate background information for their participation. The following schedule would correspond with the Lenten season:

WEEKLY SCHEDULE	PROGRAMS	PRACTICES OF FAITH
Week before Lent begins (Week of Ash Wednesday Service)	Preparing for the Journey	Ash Wednesday: Ash Wednesday
1st Week of Lent	Your Traveling Companion	Peter's Walk
2nd Week of Lent	Entering Holy Week	A Laetare Sunday
3rd Week of Lent	Arriving At The City	Making a Palm Bouquet (Option 1)
4th Week of Lent	At The Crossroads 1	The Agape Feast
5th Week of Lent	At The Crossroads 2	A Footwashing Service
6th Week of Lent (Holy Week)	The "End" of the Journey	Palm Sunday: Making a Palm Bouquet (Option 2) Holy Thursday: The Way of the Cross
Easter Sunday	Destination Easter	Holy Thursday: The Way of the Cross Youth Reaching Youth

2. Let's go on retreat!

RETREAT SCHEDULE

† † † 𝒩𝒪𝒯ℰ † † †

Use the handy publicity helps
(pages 109–112).

Friday Evening   7:30   Crowd Breakers (For a good source, use *Mudpie Olympics*.)

   8:00   Program 1: Preparing for the Journey

   9:00   Making a Lenten Bracelet

   9:30   Break

   10:00   Worship: Practice of Faith—Ash Wednesday Service

Saturday Morning   8:00   Breakfast

   9:00   Games (For a good source, use *Mudpie Olympics*)

   9:30   Program 3: Entering Holy Week

   10:30   Break

   11:00   Program 4: Arriving at the City

Saturday Afternoon   Noon   Lunch/Break

   2:00   Practice of Faith: A Laetare Sunday

   3:00   Program 6: At the Crossroads 2 Immediately followed by Practice of the Faith: Footwashing Service

   4:30   Break

   5:30   Program 5: At the Crossroads 1

Saturday Evening   6:30   Dinner/Worship: The Agape Feast

   8:00   Break

   9:00   Program 7: The "End" of the Journey

   10:00   Practice of Faith: The Way of the Cross (Youth leaders should prepare this experience for youth in advance.)

Sunday Morning   8:00   Breakfast

   9:00   Program 8: Destination Easter

   10:00   End in worship:
Pray
Sing
Faith share about weekend

USING THE
Newsletters

This book contains nine newsletters (pages 91–108) that you can copy and mail out to all of the youth, not just to the participants in this Lenten study. Each newsletter contains a devotional that goes along with the week's study, a "Crazy Lenten Fact," and a "Read Ahead" section. It also has a large blank spot for "Notes From Your Fearless Leader" where you can personalize the newsletter. Use this spot to write one note to the entire group on one photocopy, then make enough photocopies for each youth; or do all of the photocopies first and then write a personal note to each youth.

Using the newsletter helps you
† get the word out;
† generate enthusiasm for the experiences;
† challenge young persons to greater spiritual discipline during Lent;
† connect personally with the youth during the week.

USING THE
Journal

"ALONG THE PATH, A COMPANION FOR THE JOURNEY"

On pages 82–90 is a master for creating a journal. Photocopy enough for each participant. Each page of the journal covers one of the eight sessions within the Lenten study. Encourage the youth to answer the three questions each week. The questions give the participants a chance to integrate the information into their life.

The participants can decide to do one question a day, all three at once, or all three several times throughout the week. Flexibility is the key.

USING THE
Publicity Helps

See you there · · · · · · · · · · ·
Your information here!

On pages 109–112 are handy posters to help you publicize the various programs and practices. Photocopy them as part of your youth newsletters; post copies in the youth meeting areas and in the church; mail them out to the youth. On the posters, fill in the specifics of time, date, and location. Be sure to also send them out to youth who are related to the church but who are not active in youth group or Sunday school. This type of event or short-term program may be just the opportunity that draws them into greater involvement in the life of your church.

---

† † † *NOTE* † † †

Don't forget to mail each week's newsletters (pages 91–108) to all of the youth.

Youth like to get mail!

† † † *NOTE* † † †

Make copies of the journal for the youth (pages 82–90).

† † † *NOTE* † † †

Encourage participants to bring their friends; make this season a time of reaching new youth with the Good News of Christ's great love for them.

PLANNING *Ahead*

Coordinate With Your Church Calendar

When planning for your Lenten study, be sure that your program is coordinated with your church calendar. For instance, you don't want to plan a special Ash Wednesday service for the youth only to find that there is a churchwide service at the same time.

Use this study as an opportunity to involve volunteer adult leaders with your program. It would be especially appropriate at this time to have your pastor involved in some of the programs.

There are also some Practices of the Faith that lend themselves quite well to adults. It would be a good opportunity to provide a churchwide program, or a program involving youth and their parents.

Gather Your Supplies

Basic Supplies

Bibles, paper, pencils, pens, markers, hymnals, chalkboard and chalk or dry-erase board and dry-erase markers, large sheets of paper

† NOTE † † †

It is important to check this supply list in advance. While some items are readily available, some will take time to secure.

FOR THE PROGRAMS

Program 1—Preparing for the Journey
- ❏ Newspapers or magazines
- ❏ Copies of the handout "Making a Lenten Sackcloth Bracelet" (pages 18–19)
- ❏ Natural colored burlap (You can make approximately 50 bracelets from one yard of burlap.) Burlap is available from fabric or discount stores that carry fabrics.
- ❏ Velcro® strips about ¾-inch long
- ❏ *Optional:* Gray embroidery floss. (You can make 20 bracelets from a 25-yard skein.) Embroidery floss is sold at discount or fabric stores.
- ❏ *Optional:* Large-eyed needles (one per youth)
- ❏ *Optional: Ragman and Other Cries of Faith,* by Walter Wangerin, Jr. (Harper San Francisco, 1994)

Program 2—Your Traveling Companion
- ❏ Copies of the handout "John: The Disciple Whom Jesus Loved" (page 25)

Program 3—Entering Holy Week
- ❏ Copies of the handout "The Passion of Christ—The Passion of the People" (pages 30–31)

❏ Copies of the handout "Making and Accepting Apologies" (page 32)
❏ *Optional:* Cupcake (Pax Cake) for each youth

Program 4—Arriving at the City
❏ Copies of the handout "Four Ways of Dealing With Anger" (pages 38–39)
❏ Copies of "A Prayer of St. Francis of Assisi" (page 37)

Program 5—At the Crossroads 1
❏ *Optional:* Communion cup and plate

Program 6—At the Crossroads 2
❏ Good-humored volunteer to play a leper
❏ Old clothes large enough to fit over "the leper's" clothes. Clothes should be as dirty and ragged as you can get them.
❏ White glue mixed with non-toxic tempera paint to the color of a reddish sore
❏ Large towel

❏ Basin and pitcher of water
❏ Whole egg mixed with a small amount of brown tempera paint
❏ Pair of tweezers
❏ Toothpick
❏ Dark dirt (such as potting soil)
❏ *Optional:* WWJD? Bracelets for each participant. Bracelets are available in cloth for around $1.50 at most Christian bookstores.

Program 7—The "End" of the Journey
❏ Copies of the handout "Jesus' Suffering and Death" (page 52)
❏ Leather belt
❏ Small piece of thorn branch for each youth
❏ Large nail for each youth
❏ *Optional:* Cross in My Pocket (card and cross) for each youth. These are available through most Christian book stores for between 25 and 50 cents apiece.

Program 8—Destination Easter
❏ Copies of handout "Jesus Road" (page 55)

† FOR PRACTICES OF FAITH

† † † NOTE † † †

The Ash Wednesday service will be most effective if used as written. However, if you are unable to burn cards, ashes can be ordered through your local Christian bookstore.

Ash Wednesday Service
❏ Fireproof container/grate for burning cards and palms
❏ Large candle and small candle for lighting cards and palms
❏ Small container to mix ashes in
❏ Small container of water to add to ashes
❏ Scoop or spoon for transferring ashes
❏ Towel for leader to clean hands
❏ Card and pencil for each participant
❏ A small amount of dried palms. If these are not available from the last year's Palm Sunday service, a local florist can provide a substitute. You will need to purchase the palms ahead of time to allow them to dry out.

❏ Music: A copy of the words to "Sanctuary" (from *Youth! Praise 2*) if you are not familiar with the song.
❏ Music: A copy of the song "Grace" from Wes King's CD *A Room Full of Stories*.

Peter's Walk
❏ Blindfold for each participant
❏ Rope (long enough for the entire group to hold at one time)
❏ Persons to act as guides
❏ Flashlights
❏ Baskets
❏ Pieces of bread
❏ Pieces of cooked fish
❏ Water
❏ Trash bags
❏ Towels

- Rocks
- Tape recording of a little girl, or a girl who has volunteered to read the part.
- Chairs
- Bowls of warm water
- Hammer
- Board
- Bread
- Grape juice
- Singer for "Were You There?"

A Laetare Sunday
- Lots of fun games. (Make sure to check in advance for any supplies you may need when picking the games.)
- Lots of praise songs, if you decide to have a praise worship
- Refreshments

Making a Palm Bouquet
- Six-inch (or larger) plastic foam ball, one for each bouquet
- Floral pins
- Spanish Moss (This is packaged very compactly and goes a lot farther than you would think)
- ⅛-inch to ¼-inch ribbon (satin or shiny paper) in purple, royal blue, and gold
- ¼-inch to ⁵/₁₆-inch-by-36-inch dowel or large sticks of about the same size
- Silk or fresh greens and flowers (see "Making a Palm Bouquet," pages 70–72, for suggestions).
- Photocopies of "Easter Legends of Flowers and Trees" (page 71)

The Agape Feast
- Make arrangements with your pastor to serve as the elder of this feast.
- Food: fresh fruit, fish (fish sticks work well), cheeses cut into bite-size pieces. You can also use bread and soup.
- Bread and grape juice for Communion
- *Optional:* Low tables—These can be made with a piece of plywood (or fold-up tables with the legs folded in) on top of four concrete block legs.

A Footwashing Service
- Basin or bowl
- Pitcher of water
- Towel
- Chair for each person
- Music: A copy of the words to "Sanctuary" (*Youth! Praise 2*) if you are not familiar with the song, a copy of the words to "From the Rising of the Sun," soft instrumental music to play during the actual footwashing
- Plans for immediate service project and transportation for youth
- *Optional:* WWJD? bracelets for those who did not receive them during Program 6

The Way of the Cross
- This Practice of Faith has many options (see pages 77–81). Plan early with your youth to be sure that all of the supplies needed are available.
- Photocopies of the handouts on pages 79–81

†††𝒩𝒪𝒯ℰ†††

Note: If you are making palm bouquets of silk flowers, they can be made ahead of time. If you are using fresh flowers, they will need to be made right before the worship service. All of the supplies listed (with the exception of greens and flowers) are available at craft stores or discount stores that carry craft supplies.

Youth Reaching Youth—A natural follow up to this study is the practice of faith-sharing.
Youth Reaching Youth and the student resource *Turning Points* will help youth reach out to others with the Good News of Christ's love.
(Available from Abingdon Press at your local Christian bookstore.)

HOLY WEEK Journey

Palm Sunday: The Passion Begins

The people honor Jesus—for now!

Cleansing the Temple

Jesus drives out dishonest moneychangers, who dishonor the worship of God.

The disciples listen, although they do not yet understand. The chief priests plot to kill Jesus. To them, he is a troublemaker.

Jesus Teaching

Easter Sunday: *Resurrection!*

Death cannot keep the Son of God. He lives!
Jesus Christ is risen.

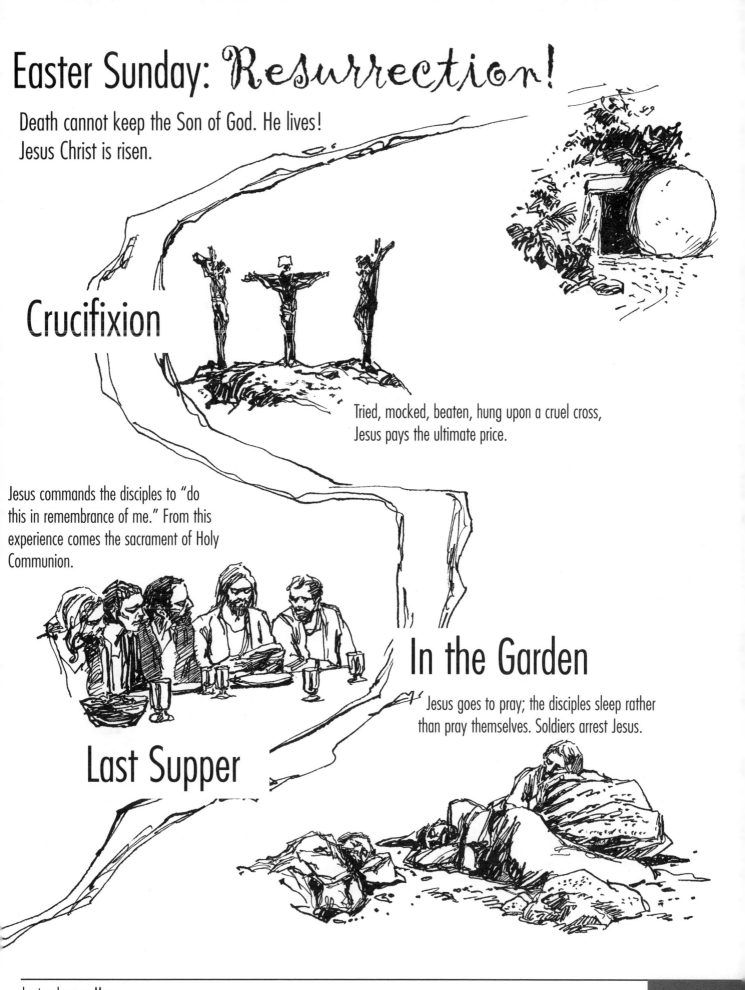

Crucifixion

Tried, mocked, beaten, hung upon a cruel cross,
Jesus pays the ultimate price.

Jesus commands the disciples to "do
this in remembrance of me." From this
experience comes the sacrament of Holy
Communion.

In the Garden

Jesus goes to pray; the disciples sleep rather
than pray themselves. Soldiers arrest Jesus.

Last Supper

PREPARING FOR
the Journey

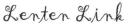

Lenten Link

Lent is a time of examining our life, of confessing our sin, and of repenting and returning to the Christ way. Ash Wednesday, the first day of Lent, emphasizes repentance.

Focus

To introduce youth to the idea of turning away from sin and starting again.

Practice of Faith

Ash Wednesday Service (pages 56–58)

Scripture

Daniel 9:3 and 2 Corinthians 5:17

(10–15 minutes)   *Ash Wednesday*

Invite the youth to work in pairs or teams for 4 or 5 minutes to come up with as much information as they can about Lent. You may make this exercise either cooperative or competitive. Its purpose is to engage the youth in beginning to think about the Lenten season. It will also give you an idea of how much they already know. (See "Ten Questions Youth Will Ask," pages 4–5, for background.)

Bring the conversation around to focus on Ash Wednesday. What do the youth know about this observance? Here are some key concepts and definitions to bring out during the discussion:

† **Ash Wednesday** is a time when we confront our mortality and confess our sins before God, within a community of faith like a youth group, small group, or Bible study group. It is a chance to look at sin and death in the light of the redeeming love of Jesus Christ.

† **Ashes** have often been used as a sign of mortality and repentance. In the past, those seeking Christ and forgiveness would approach the church altar and have the sign of the cross placed on their head as a sign of repentance. The ashes provided a nonverbal and experiential way of participating in the call to repentance and reconciliation.

† Mortality: The condition of being subject to death. Humans are mortal.

† Repentance: Expressing sorrow for and willingness to change actions, thoughts, or attitudes that are out of line with Christ's teaching. To repent is to ask forgiveness and to turn around.

† Reconciliation: Restoring relationship. Christ's death and resurrection removed the barrier of sin to bring people back into a right relationship with God. Christ's spirit also helps persons be reconciled to one another.

What Is Sin?

(15–20 minutes)

Supplies
Chalkboard, dry-erase board, or large sheets of paper; chalk or marker; pencils or pens and paper; newspapers and magazines

Ask the youth to define the word *sin*. Again, they may work in pairs or teams. Or have them each write a definition and post their statements on the wall. Here are some examples of what other people say sin is:

> † "Falling short of God's glory." —Angie, age 18

> † "Anything that harms someone or offends someone is a sin— because it causes a barrier." —Wayne, 60

> † "Doing something against the Bible that I know is wrong." —Rebecca, 24

> † "Sin is disobeying God." —Jordan, 12

> † "Sin is the closed door, the turned off light. Sin is the opposite of true happiness." —Lara, 12

Here are two "official" definitions:

> † "Missing the mark of God's will by choice and because of human weakness. Action or attitude that disobeys or betrays God or that fails to do good. Sin always brings pain" (*Holman Student Bible Dictionary*).

> † Going against "religious or moral law, especially when deliberate. Deliberate disobedience to the known will of God. A condition of estrangement from God resulting from such disobedience" (*The American Heritage Dictionary*).

Challenge the youth to see who can list on paper the most sins in two minutes. Handout recent newspapers and magazines for the youth to check for sin that jumps out of the headlines. (This way the sins the youth list are not just personal sins.)

On the left side of a large sheet of paper, chalkboard, or dry-erase board, list the sins the youth have identified. Then draw a vertical line down the center, and write *God* in large letters on the other side of it. This line visually represents the fact that sin separates us from God. (See next page.)

THE CONSEQUENCES OF SIN

SINS
(List of Sins)

God

Here is another way to illustrate this concept:

Say: "When we are in a relationship with God, we are in direct conversation."

(*Face those present and establish direct eye contact with them. As you talk, slowly raise a notebook, paper, or other large item in front of your face.*)

"When we sin, it's as if a wall stands between us and God; it blocks our direct contact. God is still there, but our unconfessed sins keep us from being together."

(*Your face should be completely obscured.*)

"When we confess and repent of our sins, the wall falls away; and we can see God again, face to face."

(*Remove the notebook, paper, or other large item, and again establish direct eye contact with those present.*)

"Sins not only separate us from God but also from other people. Sins also have other consequences." Give some examples, such as these:

  † Lying to your parents can result in a loss of privileges.
  † Cheating on a test can result in a feeling of guilt or if a teacher catches you, in a failing grade.
  † Gossiping can result in hurting a friend or even ending a relationship.

Take a moment in silence after asking the youth (and yourself) the following:

  † Is there anything in your life that is separating you from God?

(10–15 minutes)

God's Grace

Supplies
Optional: Ragman and Other Cries of Faith, by Walter Wangerin, Jr. (Harper San Francisco, 1994)

Say: "While all sins have different consequences, all sins are equal in the eyes of God. And yes, while there are consequences, if we honestly seek God's forgiveness, all of our sins will be erased and forgotten. We call this grace."

If you were using a dry-erase board or chalkboard, erase the sins and the line. Instead of the word *sin*, replace it with the word *you*; and draw a line connecting *you* and *God* to show the relationship.

If you were using paper, tear it up. Have the youth tear up their lists of sins as well. On a fresh paper, write *you* and *God* and connect them.

YOU ◄─────► GOD

Say: "By turning away from sin and seeking forgiveness (repentance), we are truly forgiven of the past by God. We call this justification."

✝ **Justification:** God's act of bringing a repentant person back into a right relationship with God. Think of *justification* as "just-as-if-I-had-not-sinned."

✝ **Grace:** God's free and undeserved love, which never quits.

Read the story "Ragman," from *Ragman and Other Cries of Faith,* by Walter Wangerin, Jr., to explain God's grace and forgiveness further. While you are reading, have the youth close their eyes. Ask them to visualize what is happening in the story. At the end of the story ask youth to write their definition of grace.

Sackcloth Reminders

(20–30 minutes)

Read Daniel 9:3.

Supplies
Bibles, copies of instructions for making Sackcloth Bracelets (pages 18–19)

Tell the youth that during Bible times, wearing coarse or uncomfortable sackcloth instead of ordinary cloth was a sign of repentance for sinful acts.

Invite the youth to wear the bracelet until the end of Lent as a reminder to seek forgiveness for sins, which separate us from a relationship with God.

Hand out copies of the instructions for the Sackcloth bracelets.

✝ **Sackcloth:** Rough clothing worn as a sign grief for the dead, repentance over personal sin, or sorrow over disaster. Sackcloth was made of goat or camel hair. It covered the middle of the body or the whole body.

Pray together

(2 minutes)

Draw everyone together. Encourage them to keep their Lenten journals (see pages 82–90) and to participate in the other Lenten observances of your church.

Supplies
Bible; copies of the Lenten journals for each person (pages 82–90)

Summarize the Ash Wednesday focus on repentance and then offer words of assurance from **2 Corinthians 5:17.** Close with the following prayer:

Gracious and loving God,
We confess that we have allowed things to separate us from you. We ask your forgiveness. We give thanks for the assurance of your forgiveness; we rejoice in your grace. Help us this week to walk more closely with you each day. Amen

MAKING A LENTEN
Sackcloth Bracelet

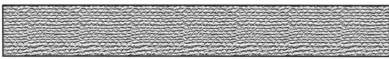

1. Cut a piece of burlap 1 inch to 1½ inches wide by 10 inches long.

2. Pull two 10-inch strings out of each of the long edges. Discard these.

3. Cut a piece of Velcro® ¾-inch long. Keep the pieces stuck together for now. Remove one of the backing papers from the Velcro® and place the Velcro® on the end of what will be the outside of your bracelet.

4. Get help from a friend to wrap your bracelet around your wrist. (*Be careful not to wrap it too tightly!*) Remove the other backing paper from the Velcro®, and press on your bracelet to secure the Velcro® and to finish the bracelet closure. (*When you remove the bracelet, you will see that the Velcro® is on the outside of one end of the bracelet and on the inside of the other end.*)

Velcro® on outside

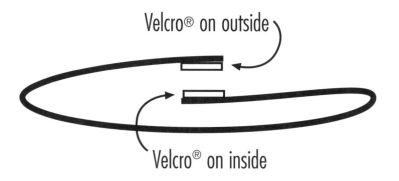

Velcro® on inside

5. Cut off any excess bracelet length.

Congratulations! You have made a bracelet.

If you wish to embroider a cross on your bracelet, remove the bracelet and complete steps 6–13.

6. Cut a 15-inch length of embroidery floss. (*You'll notice that there are several strands of thread. Do not separate the strands! You'll need to use all of them.*)

7. Thread the needle. Tie a knot in one end of the thread.

8. If you look closely at the bracelet, the fabric looks something like this. Decide where you want to cross-stitch the cross.

9. At the bottom of where the cross will be, insert the needle from the back through a hole. Then stick the needle into the burlap, forming ½ of an X.

10. Pull the needle through the opposite corner (3) and back down through the burlap (4). You have formed an *X*.

11. Continue in the same way until you have made 9 Xs.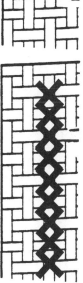

12. Count down to the 4th X. Add 3 Xs on each side of the center line.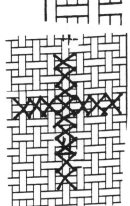

13. Remove the needle. Tie a knot in the thread. Cut off the extra thread. You're done!

YOUR TRAVELING
Companion: John

Lenten Link

John, sometimes referred to as the Beloved Disciple, was a close companion to Jesus as he experienced the events of Holy Week, which we commemorate during Lent.

Focus

To help youth discover that they are a lot like John and that Jesus loved John regardless of his faults.

Practice of Faith

Peter's Walk (pages 59–65)

Scripture

2 Corinthians 5:17

(10–15 minutes)

Who Was John?

Supplies

Chalkboard, dry-erase board, or large sheets of paper; chalk or marker; Bibles; copies of the handout "John: The Disciple Whom Jesus Loved" (page 25)

† † † NOTE † † †

If you plan to do "Peter's Walk" (pages 59–65), have the youth put a star next to the Scriptures where Peter was also present. Also, explain that James was John's brother.

John is referred to as "the disciple whom Jesus loved" six times in the Book of John. In studying the Gospels, you will find that Jesus was very fond of John and trusted him. Let's find out what he was like.

Distribute the "John—The Disciple Whom Jesus Loved" handout. Instruct the youth to look up the Scriptures and answer the questions. When they have completed their worksheets, review their answers, using the information below. (A star (✫) indicates when Peter was also present.)

Mark 5:35-43 ✫—John witnessed the raising of Jairus' daughter from the dead. In verse 43, Jesus trusted John not to tell anyone.

Matthew 17:1-9 ✫—Jesus included John as a witness of the miracle of the Transfiguration. In verse 9, Jesus trusted John not to tell anyone.

Mark 13:3-37 ✫—Jesus trusted John enough to reveal to him about the end of the age.

Luke 22:7-8 ✫—Jesus trusted John with making the preparations for the Passover meal.

John 13:23 ✶—John had a place of prominence, sitting next to Jesus at the Last Supper.

Mark 14:32-33 ✶—Jesus chose John to support him and witness his agony in the Garden of Gethsemane.

John 19:25-27—John was the only disciple at the cross. All of the others had run away. Peter had denied him three times. Jesus chose John to care for his mother, which he did until her death.

John 20:1-10 ✶—John was one of the first to see the empty tomb.

You may want to add that in chapters 20 and 21 of John, it is recorded that Jesus appeared three times to the disciples. Each time, John was present. John was also present at Pentecost and was active in the early church.

Reveal the answers for the five books that are traditionally attributed to John. Give the additional information.

1. The Gospel of John—**Read John 20:21** to find out why John wrote this book.
2. First John—This letter has at least five purposes: to promote fellowship, to produce happiness, to protect holiness, to promote Christian beliefs, and to provide hope.
3. Second John—The basic theme in this letter is a reminder to continue to love one another.
4. Third John—This letter encourages fellowship with other Christians.
5. The Book of Revelation—This book focuses on the age to come and gives a message of hope for believers.

JOHN WAS TRULY A REMARKABLE MAN!

Will the Real John Please Stand Up?

(15–20 minutes)

Ask:
- † What kind of mental picture do you have of John when he was called by Christ to be a disciple?
- † What did he look like?
- † How old do you think he was?
- † What kind of a person do you think he was?
- † What were his personality traits?

† † † NOTE † † †

If you will be doing "Peter's Walk," tell the youth that Peter was also very special to Jesus. While Peter's time with Jesus was similar, it was also unique. Invite the youth to learn more about Peter and his walk with Christ by participating in "Peter's Walk" (pages 59–65).

Supplies
Bibles

† † † *NOTE* † † †

Assign the Scriptures in the next two sections to various youth to look up and read at the appropriate time.

† † † *NOTE* † † †

Do not expect a verbal answer to every question in these sections. At times, silence is OK. Just pause a few seconds and move on.

Combine input from the youth and write a general description of how they picture John. They will probably describe an elderly, bearded man who is very sincere, kind, and loving.

Challenge the youth by saying: "Now, let's search the Scriptures to see if your description is accurate." Assign the Scriptures below to youth to look up and read at the appropriate time.

List fact headings on left side of a chalkboard or dry-erase board as you talk about each of them:

Fact 1—John was an ORDINARY TEENAGER

The disciples are usually portrayed as being older men with beards and long robes. But evidence is that John was in his early teens when he was called to follow Jesus. His family did not have wealth; he worked as a fisherman. He was pretty much an average young guy of the times.

Fact 2—John was a HOTHEAD

Read Mark 3:17. "Son of Thunder" means "having the quality of thunder." John and his brother, James, were given this name because they lost their temper easily. How's your temper? Could you ever be called a "Son or Daughter of Thunder"?

Fact 3—John was EXCLUSIVE

Read Luke 9:49. John thought the disciples were better than anyone else. Do you ever exclude people?

Fact 4—John was JUDGMENTAL

Read Luke 9:51-54. Because they were rejected, John wanted to destroy the town. When someone rejects you or hurts your feelings, is your first reaction ever to get even?

Fact 5—John was SELFISH

Read Mark 10:35-37 and Matthew 20:20-21. Jesus tried time and time again to tell the disciples what was going to happen to him. But they did not understand. They thought that he was going to set up an earthly kingdom. If so, John wanted to get his bid in first, looking for the best the new kingdom had to offer to him. His mother even asked on behalf of him and his brother! Do you sometimes feel superior to other people?

Fact 6—John was GUTSY

Read John 13:23. Obviously, John was not timid; and the other disciples knew this. Do people ever look to you to be the one to try something first?

So here you have the real John. He was

† A Teenager	† A Hothead	† Selfish
† Ordinary	† Exclusive	† Gutsy
	† Judgmental	

Jesus could have selected anyone else in the world. Why do you think he chose John?

Life With Jesus Makes a Difference

As you talk about the characteristics below, list them on the board parallel to the previous headings as illustrated.

Read Matthew 4:21-22. In this Scripture, John made the decision to follow Jesus. After making this decision, his walk with Jesus became transforming. Let's see how God worked through John.

On being a TEENAGER

When Jesus asked John to follow him, John was in his teens. Does Christ still ask teens to follow him today?

Read 1 Timothy 4:12. How can this Scripture be applied to your life?

On being ORDINARY

In the Book of Acts, Peter and John are together when Peter healed a crippled beggar. They were brought before the Sanhedrin (Jewish ruling body) to be questioned. Filled with the Holy Spirit, Peter spoke.

Read Acts 4:13. The Scripture tells that they were unschooled, ordinary men. Can you think of a time in the Bible when God used anything but ordinary people? With God, the

Ordinary - - - - - - - becomes - - - - - - - Extraordinary

On being a HOTHEAD

Apparently Jesus was not disturbed by the hothead emotions of John. Perhaps because where there is strong emotion, there is power. Hot anger can be destructive; but under the control of Christ it turns into a strong constructive force.

Destructive Anger - - - - - - becomes - - - - - - Constructive

What examples of potentially destructive reactions can you think of? How can they be used constructively?

On being EXCLUSIVE

Read 1 John 4:18-21. This Scripture was written by John later in life. In what way did Jesus change John's heart?

Exclusive - - - - - - - - becomes - - - - - - - - Inclusive

On being JUDGMENTAL

Read Luke 6:37-38 (Jesus' teaching).
Read 3 John 5-7 (how John was changed).

Judgmental - - - - - - - - becomes - - - - - - - - Understanding

In what ways do we judge others? How can we turn judgment into understanding?

On being SELFISH

Read 1 John 3:16-18.

Selfish - - - - - - - - becomes - - - - - - - - Giving

How are we selfish in our lives? How can we become more giving?

On being GUTSY

Is having a lot of nerve a bad characteristic or a good characteristic? Give some examples of how having a lot of nerve can be both good and bad.

Gutsy- - - - - - - - - -becomes - - - - - - - -Courageous

(3 minutes)

Me? A Follower of Jesus?

Ask: Do you sometimes feel you have nothing to offer God? that there's nothing good about you?

Read 2 Corinthians 5:17.

Because John decided to follow Christ, he truly became a new creation. Jesus loves you too—more than you can ever imagine. Like John, you too have a decision to make: Will you follow Christ?

End in prayer, naming each youth individually, asking Christ to help them become a new creation.

JOHN: The Disciple Whom Jesus Loved

Look up the following Scriptures and find out what happened with John on each of these occasions:

Mark 5:35-43—What did John witness? _____

In Verse 43, what did Jesus trust John not to do? _____

Matthew 17:1-9—What did John witness? _____

In Verse 9, what did Jesus trust John not to do? _____

Mark 13:3-37—What did Jesus reveal to John? _____

Luke 22:7-8—What did Jesus trust John to do? _____

John 13:23—John had a place of prominence. Where was he? _____

Mark 14:32-33—What did Jesus choose John to do? _____

John 19:25-27—Who was the only disciple at the cross? _____

What did Jesus trust John to do? _____

John 20:1-9—John was one of the first to see what? _____

John is traditionally credited with writing five books of the Bible. Can you name them?

1. _____

2. _____

3. _____

4. _____

5. _____

BEGINNING THE JOURNEY
Through Holy Week

Lenten Link

One of the emphases of Lent is seeking forgiveness and reconciling or making peace with persons who may have wronged us or whom we may have wronged.

Focus

To help youth develop the necessary skills for apologizing and accepting apologies.

Practice of Faith
Palm Bouquets (pages 70–72)

Scripture
Luke 19:28-38

(6–10 minutes)

Supplies

Chalkboard, dry-erase board, or large sheets of paper; chalk or markers Bibles; copies of the handout "The Passion of Christ—The Passion of the People" (pages 30–31); copies of the handout "Making and Accepting Apologies" (page 32)

Optional: Pax Cake (cupcake) for each youth

Palm Sunday or Passion Sunday?

Read aloud Luke 19:28-38. Read aloud or explain in your own words the following:

Palm Sunday, the beginning of Holy Week, is a day of joy when we celebrate Christ's triumphal entry into the city of Jerusalem. It was then that the crowds threw down articles of clothing, waved palm branches, and proclaimed Jesus their king. Palm Sunday is usually celebrated in church services with a palm procession and the singing of hosannas.

Passion Sunday is another name for Palm Sunday. Although they are the same day, the terms and focus of Palm Sunday and Passion Sunday are quite different. Where Palm Sunday focuses on the joy of the day, Passion Sunday focuses on Christ's passion or suffering. It is important that we not let the celebration of Palm Sunday crowd out the observation of Passion Sunday, because it is in the Passion where the true story lies.

Write the word *passion* on a chalkboard or dry-erase board; explain two different meanings of passion:

Passion, when used with Christ, refers to his suffering.

Passion can also be extreme emotion, such as love and hate.

Together do the reading on the handout "The Passion of Christ—The Passion of the People" (pages 30–31). Then discuss the following questions:

✝ You were there. You were part of the crowd. What were you feeling in each scene?

✝ Later you came to realize that Jesus was indeed the Messiah, the Son of God. Think back to Jesus' words on the cross. How does recalling them make you feel about your participation in the crowd?

✝ After the Resurrection, Jesus appeared to two travelers on the road to Emmaus. If you, as part of the crowd, were on that road also and encountered Jesus, what is the one thing you would want to say? (*I'm sorry; forgive me.*)

✝ What do you think his answer would have been?

Making and Accepting an Apology

(10 minutes)

Two important teachings of Jesus were love (Mark 12:31) and forgiveness (Matthew 18:21-22). We love each other because he loves us, and we forgive each other because he forgives us.

When we ask forgiveness from God, we confess our wrong doings. When we ask forgiveness from a person, we are apologizing. Accepting forgiveness from a person is accepting an apology.

Have the youth define giving and accepting an apology. Record their responses for all to see. If the responses shown in italics are not given, you may want to add them yourself.

Apologizing is . . .
(*Telling someone you are sorry for something you've done wrong; taking responsibility for a mistake.*)

When should you apologize?
(*When an action or words turn to hurt; when you have done something wrong that you are sorry for.*)

Accepting an apology is . . .
(*Forgiving the other person*)

Why should we accept an apology and forgive?
(*Because Christ forgave us. Not forgiving and becoming bitter can eat away at both the soul and the body.*)

Giving and accepting apologies do not come naturally. Both can be humbling experiences.

✝✝✝ NOTE ✝✝✝

Although it may seem simple, giving and accepting apologies is a learned skill, not something that comes naturally. Many young people have not had the opportunity to learn these skills. For those who have, the activities here should prove to be a

Distribute the "Making and Accepting Apologies" handout (page 32).
Review the points. Assign partners. Have them practice for a few minutes
giving and accepting apologies.

(8–15 minutes)

Who Needs to Apologize?

Present the following case studies. Assign two youth to each study. Have
them determine who should apologize and why. Then have them
demonstrate making and accepting an apology.

CASE 1

Lara and Kelly are good friends. Lara loaned Kelly her new blouse to wear
to the school dance. A few weeks later, Kelly had not returned the blouse; so
Lara called and asked her to return it. Kelly said that she had loaned the
blouse to someone else. Lara thought that Kelly had no right to loan out
something that did not belong to her; she let Kelly know it. Being good
friends with Kelly, Lara knew how self-conscious Kelly was about wearing
braces. So she ended the conversation by telling Kelly to go and brush her
teeth with a scouring pad and hung up the phone.

*(Lara should apologize to Kelly because her words were intentionally hurtful. Kelly
should apologize to Lara for not respecting her property when she loaned the blouse
to someone else without asking.)*

CASE 2

Blake and Duane were eating lunch together at school. Blake accidentally
spilled his carton of milk into Duane's lap. The startled look on Duane's face
made Blake laugh uncontrollably. Duane responded by dumping his carton
of milk over Blake's head. Both stormed out of the cafeteria in anger.

*(Duane should apologize to Blake, because he dumped the milk on Blake's head out
of anger. Also, Blake should apologize for spilling the milk on Duane's lap, even
though it was an accident, and for laughing about it, even if it was in response to
Duane's startled look.)*

(5–15 minutes)

The Pax Cake

In England, until recent times, there was a Palm Sunday custom of the Pax
Cake. (*Pax* is Latin for "peace." Because people did not want to go to their
Easter service with anger in their hearts, they sought out persons they had
quarreled with and offered them a Pax Cake as a token of apology. On
giving the Pax Cake, they would say, "Peace and good will," and resolve
their disagreement.

Distribute a Pax Cake to each youth. Challenge them to give their Pax Cake to someone to whom they owe an apology. Remind them to end the apology by saying, "Peace and good will."

Pass the Peace

(4 minutes)

The Peace is an ancient and traditional practice of Christian greeting. This can be done with an embrace, a handshake, or a hand clasp and the exchange of a word of blessing. The traditional words are "The peace of Christ be with you" with the other person responding, "And also with you."

Invite your youth to Pass the Peace.

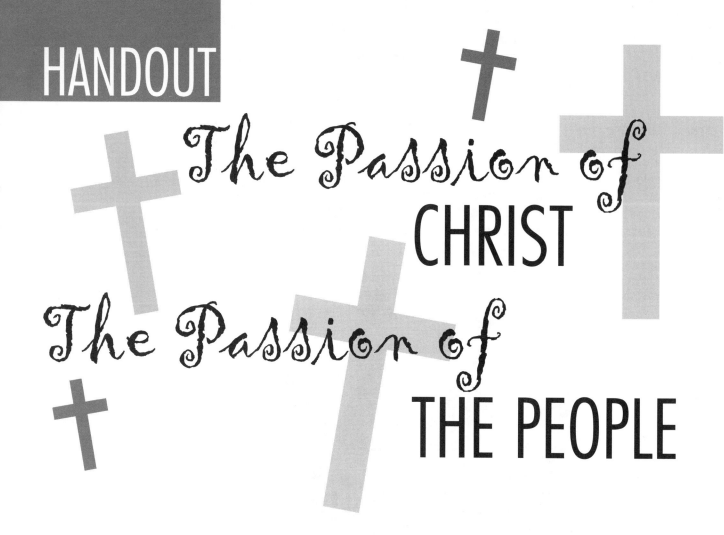

The Passion of CHRIST
The Passion of THE PEOPLE

Assign volunteers to read the parts: Reader 1, Pilate, Leaders (1 or 2), and Jesus. Everyone else is the Crowd.

As you hear the scenes read, try to visualize yourself as a person in the crowd.

Scene 1

Reader 1: Hear from the gospel of John: The next day a large crowd was in Jerusalem for Passover. When they heard that Jesus was coming for the festival, they took palm branches and went out to greet him. They shouted,

Reader 1: Hosanna to the Son of David!

Crowd: Hosanna in the highest!

Reader 1: Blessed is the One who comes in the name of the Lord.

Crowd: Hosanna in the highest!

Scene 2

Reader 1: Later that same week, the crowd was again gathered to see Jesus. But this time they were listening to the Roman governor, Pilate.

Pilate: What am I to do with Jesus, who is called the Messiah?

Crowd: (*yelling*) Nail him to a cross!

Pilate: But what crime has he done?

Crowd: (*yelling louder*) Nail him to a cross!

Pilate: I won't have anything to do with killing this man. You are the ones doing it!

Crowd: (*yelling louder*) Nail him to a cross!

Scene 3

Reader 1: The crowd gathered yet a third time that week. This time at Calvary, the place where criminals and persons accused of treason were executed on crosses. While the crowd stood there watching Jesus, the soldiers gambled for his clothes. The leaders insulted him.

Leaders (*insultingly*): He saved others. Now he should save himself—if he really is God's chosen Messiah!

Jesus: Father, forgive these people! They don't know what they're doing!

(Based on John 12:12-13a, Matthew 27:22-25, Luke 23:34-35 (CEV); *The United Methodist Book of Worship*, page 339.)

MAKING AND Accepting Apologies

Making an Apology

Look at the person.

Use a serious, sincere voice tone; but don't pout!

Begin by saying, "I wanted to apologize for . . . ," or "I'm sorry for. . . ."

Apologize for a specific mistake not for being a bad person.

Do not make excuses or give rationalizations.

Apologies are most effective when backed up with action.

Accepting an Apology

Look at the person who is apologizing.

Listen to what he or she has to say.

Put yourself in the other person's shoes. Remain calm. Refrain from any sarcastic statements.

Thank the person for the apology; say, "Thanks for saying, 'I'm sorry,' " or "That's OK."

Apologize for what you did wrong that could have also led to hurt.

From Teaching *Social Skills to Youth,* by Tom Dowd and Jeff Tierney (Boys Town Press, 1992). Used with permission.

ARRIVING AT THE CITY: Cleansing of the Temple

Lenten Link

During the week before the Crucifixion, Jesus saw the abuse of God's Temple and became angry. He drove the moneychangers away.

Focus

To help youth recognize ways of controlling anger by following Christ's example.

Practice of Faith

Laetare Sunday (pages 66–69)

Scripture

Mark 11:11; 15-17

The Temple Marketplace in Jesus' Time

(5–10 minutes)

On Sunday, Jesus rode into Jerusalem on a donkey with shouts of "Hosanna!" Following this triumphal entry, he made a stop at the Temple before returning to Bethany where he was staying.

Supplies
Bible; chairs set up as booths

Read Mark 11:11. Read or explain in your own words the following:

Marketplace: A marketplace was set up in the Temple courtyard. This courtyard was the perfect place because it served as a shortcut for the people going from the Mount of Olives to the city.

Moneychangers: When pilgrims came to worship at the Temple, they were required to pay an annual tax. This tax had to be paid in the local currency. The trade of the moneychanger, therefore, was to exchange foreign currency for local currency.

Animal Sellers: The Old Testament ruled that only unblemished animals could be offered as a sacrifice at the Temple. The type of animal sacrificed depended on the status of the family. Bulls were required of the wealthy, lambs were required from those with an average income, and doves were

required from the poor. Doves were also required for purification of women and cleansing of those with certain skin diseases.

Animals brought to the Temple could easily be disapproved by priestly inspectors. Pilgrims coming to the Passover feast needed animals that they were sure would pass the inspection, so they purchased them from the animal sellers.

Reenact the Temple scene as Jesus would have seen it.

Limit the courtyard scene to a small, confined space. Assign a few youth to be moneychangers and a few to be animal sellers. Use chairs to represent their booths. If you have a large group, some could be smelly animals!

The rest of the youth are to travel from the Mount of Olives (one side of the room) to the city (the other side of the room). They will need to exchange their money, pay their tax, and purchase an animal. The moneychangers and animal sellers should try to attract the travelers' attention to trade with them.

Let the scene go on for just a few moments. Then stop the action and tell the participants that you forgot something. Explain that the Temple courtyard they used is what was known as the "Gentile's Court." In Isaiah 5:7, the Gentiles were assured that they would be allowed to worship God in the Temple. This courtyard was the only part of the Temple where the Gentiles could worship God and gather for prayer.

Assign two youth to be Gentiles. Instruct them to kneel in the middle of the marketplace and try to pray in earnest. Start the action again.

Let the action go for two to four minutes. Then stop the action and have the youth take their seats.

Jesus at the Temple

(5–10 minutes)

Supplies
Bible; chairs set up as booths

According to Mark 11:11, what did Jesus do when he entered the courtyard? (*He looked around and left.*) On Monday, Jesus returned to the Temple.

Read Mark 11:15-17.

What characters in our Temple scene was Jesus angry with and why?

† The moneychangers were cheating God's people by charging high fees for changing their money.

† The priestly inspectors and animal sellers probably worked together to cheat the people.

† The people were being disrespectful of God's Temple by using the courtyard as a shortcut.

† The Gentiles were being robbed of their right to worship.

Read John 2:13-16. Some people use this story as justification for the use of force as a response to their anger. What do you think?

Read 1 Peter 2:19-23. What does this Scripture say to you about the cleansing of the Temple? (*Jesus was angry for God's honor and God's people. When Jesus was personally abused, he said nothing.*)

Anger is an emotion. Anger is not bad. It is how we react in anger that can sometimes be wrong.

Dealing With Our Own Anger

(15–25 minutes)

Read Ephesians 4:26. What can we learn from the example Jesus set for controlling our anger?

List the responses; focus on the following:

1. **Think before you act.**
   (*Jesus did not react immediately to his anger. He thought about it and returned the next day.*)

2. **Examine your motive.**
   (*Read Philippians 2:3. Jesus' motive was love. His confrontation put himself in danger from the Sadducees.*)

Distribute pencils and paper. Give these instructions to the youth:

Controlling your anger is sometimes easier said than done. Different people respond differently to anger. Think of a time over the past few weeks when you were angry. Write down what made you angry.

Now, write down how you responded.

Think of another time when you were really angry. Write down what made you angry and how you responded.

(*Write the four categories on the chalkboard or dry-erase board.*) Depending on the circumstances, your response for both situations was probably similar and falls into one of these categories. Are you

A TIME BOMB—Explosive;

A CLAM—Holding it in;

A MARTYR—Poor me; or

AN AVENGER—Holding a grudge and getting revenge?

Supplies
Paper and pencils; copies of the handout "Four Ways of Dealing With Anger" (pages 38–39)

† † † NOTE † † †
Pause between questions for the youth to write.

Give the following examples (or your own); ask the youth to guess which category each one represents. Then ask them to place themselves into the category that seems to fit them best:

† You weren't invited to a party, but all of your friends were. You felt sorry for yourself and went home and complained to your mom. **(martyr)**

† Your dad yelled at you for something you didn't do. You turned around and kicked the cat. **(time bomb)**

† A girl has been flirting with your boyfriend. You start a rumor to get back at her. Or another guy has asked your girlfriend out. You make plans to rough him up after school. **(avenger)**

† Someone at school laughed at your new hair style. You said that it didn't bother you. **(clam)**

Divide the youth into four small groups according to their anger responses. Distribute the anger handouts (pages 38–39).

Each group is to use the suggestions there to develop two skits—one that shows an inappropriate response and its possible consequences, and the same situation with an appropriate response and its possible consequences.

Bring the groups back together to perform and talk about their skits. Suggest that they take their handouts home for future reference when they are angry.

Pray to Be Peacemakers

(5 minutes)

Supplies

Bible; copies of "A Prayer of St. Francis of Assisi" (page 37)

Summarize the session. Remind the youth that anger in itself is not bad. By following Jesus' example and his teachings, we can learn how to avoid anger or to handle anger in constructive ways.

Read Ephesians 4:30-5:2. Pray together the Prayer of St. Francis of Assisi. Encourage the youth to take home and post this prayer where they can see it often.

A PRAYER OF
St. Francis of Assisi

Lord, make me an instrument of your peace,
Where there is hatred, let me sow love;
Where there is injury, pardon;
Where there is doubt, faith;
Where is despair, hope;
Where there is darkness, light;
and where there is sadness, joy.

O Divine Master, grant that I many not so much seek
to be consoled as to console,
to be understood as to understand,
to be loved as to love.

For it is in giving that we receive,
it is in pardoning that we are pardoned,
and it is in dying that we are born to eternal life.
Amen.

FOUR WAYS OF
Dealing With Anger

THE TIME BOMB
Ready to Explode!

Tips for dealing with your anger

✝ Take 10 steps back and 10 deep breaths; or leave the situation and find a calm person to talk to; or lean up against a wall and try as hard as you can to move the wall.

✝ Remember: violence is *never* an appropriate response!

✝ Later, in a calmer mood, you may choose to talk with the person who made you angry.

Example

Don't say: Why did you gossip about me?

Do say: I felt hurt when I heard you talked about my personal problems with Susie.

Memorize the following Scripture and recite it with prayer when you're angry:

You should be quick to listen and slow to speak or get angry. If you are angry, you cannot do any of the good things that God wants done.

James 1:19-20 (CEV)

THE CLAM
Holding It In!

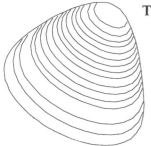

Tips for dealing with your anger

✝ Recognize that pretending that you are not angry and saying that all is fine and forgiven when it really is not will not change the person or the situation.

✝ Keeping things bottled up can lead to depression.

✝ Do not ignore your feelings. Find someone to talk to (youth workers are great for this!); or if it will help the situation, confront the person who made you angry and let your feelings be known. Say what you need to say without hurting the other person.

Example

Don't say: "Why did you gossip about me?"

Do say: "I felt hurt when I heard that you had talked about my personal problems with Susie."

Memorize the following Scripture and recite it with prayer when you're angry:

Be angry but do not sin; do not let the sun go down on your anger.

Ephesians 4:46a

THE MARTYR
Poor Me!

Tips for dealing with your anger

† Feeling sorry for yourself is usually done to get attention and to make others feel guilty.
  † Look at the situation through the other person's eyes.
  † Find an unbiased person to talk to.
  † If it will help the situation, confront the person who made you angry and let your feelings be known, saying what you need to say without hurting the other person.

Example
Don't say: Why did you gossip about me?
Do say: I felt hurt when I heard you talked about my personal problems with Susie.

Memorize the following Scripture and recite it with prayer when you're angry:

It is wise to be patient and show what you are like by forgiving others.
Proverbs 19:11 (CEV)

THE AVENGER
Get Revenge!

Tips for dealing with your anger

† You may think to get revenge, but God is the judge and avenger—not you. God says: "I'll do the punishing; you do the forgiving!"
† Look at the situation through the other person's eyes, try to find a reasonable explanation for the behavior.
† Find an unbiased person to talk to.
† If it will help the situation, confront the person who made you angry and let your feelings be known. Say what you need to say without hurting the other person.

Example
Don't say: Why did you gossip about me?
Do say: I felt hurt when I heard you talked about my personal problems with Susie.

Memorize the following Scripture and recite it with prayer when you're angry:

Only fools get angry quickly and hold a grudge.
Ecclesiastes 7:9 (CEV)

Follow Christ's example:
† Think before you act.
† Ask yourself why you are angry.
† Ask yourself if any good will come of your reaction.
† Examine your motives.
† Always act out of love, putting the needs of others ahead of your own.

Program 5

AT THE CROSSROADS:
The Last Supper

Lenten Link
Jesus ate his last meal with his disciples and gave new meaning to the covenant.

Focus
To help youth better understand the Last Supper and the sacrament of Holy Communion.

Practice of Faith
Agape Feast (pages 73–74)

Scripture
Luke 22:19-20

(2–8 minutes)

Covenant

Supplies
Bibles

Say: "During his last week, Jesus and his disciples gathered for the Passover meal. Passover celebrates the covenantal relationship between God and Israel and God's deliverance of the Israelites from slavery in Egypt. At the Last Supper together, Jesus gave the meal new meaning. But before we talk about that, let's look more at the significance of covenant and Passover."

Review this information with the youth. You may wish to use a question and answer format to engage the youth. Write out the key words.

A covenant is an agreement between two parties, defining the relationship between them. The rights, responsibilities, and obligations of each side are spelled out in the terms of this agreement. Marriage, for example, is form of covenant: Two people have agreed to "become as one," living together in a union of love, trust, and respect.

God established a covenant first with Abraham and Sarah (Genesis 17:1-8), promising to bless them with many descendants and to give the land of Canaan to them as their homeland. More important, God chose to enter into relationship with Abraham and his descendants: "I will establish my covenant between me and you, and your offspring after you throughout their generations, for an everlasting covenant, to be God to you and to your offspring after you" (Genesis 17:7).

Read Exodus 6:1-8.

God "remembers" the covenant made with Abraham. God moved to act decisively to fulfill those promises by freeing the Israelites from slavery in Egypt and leading them to the land that had been promised to Abraham.

In response to this gracious act of redemption, as their part of the covenant, the Israelites were asked to live a life of obedience and praise, worshiping only God, and to live according to the laws handed down to them at Sinai. These Ten Commandments spelled out how the people were to relate to God and to one another with justice and kindness.

Passover: A New Beginning

(4—8 minutes)

Read Exodus 12:1-30 and talk about the following information:

The people of Israel did as Moses told them to do. They ate the special meal of roasted lamb, unleavened bread (bread made without yeast), bitter herbs, and wine that evening. They painted some of the lamb's blood on the door posts of their home. The blood showed that the people had obeyed God; consequently, the angel of death "passed over" their homes, sparing the lives of the firstborn children of Israel.

Ask: "Why do you think that God asked the Israelites to mark their doors with blood? Could God really not tell which houses belonged to the Egyptians and which belonged to the Israelites?"

Remembering. Sometimes we are asked to do things not for the sake of accomplishing something, but rather, because it helps us to remember. Leaving a note to remind us to do something doesn't actually do the task, but it helps us remember to do it. In the same way, the blood of the Passover lamb that the Israelites were asked to put on their door posts served more as a reminder of God's promise to the people than a sign to direct the angel of death away from the homes of the Israelites.

Blood is a symbol of life, and was a sign to the Israelites both that God had spared their lives and also a sign of the new life that they were about to begin. In the deepest sense, the lamb's blood was a sign of God's covenant with Israel.

The Passover meal and the deliverance of the Israelites marked not only the beginning of a new relationship with God, but they also signaled a radical change in the identity of the Israelites: They were no longer the people that would be known as slaves serving the Egyptians, but rather as a free people serving God, who had saved them from bondage. This meal and even the particular month that it occurred in (see Verse 2) marked a new beginning for the Israelite people.

Since that time, Jewish families have celebrated the Passover each year by eating a special meal of lamb, unleavened bread, wine, and other

Supplies
Bibles

At the first Passover, God made a pledge to the Israelites to be their God and to deliver them from captivity in Egypt.

symbolic foods. This meal, called the Seder, serves as a reminder of the covenant between God and the Jewish people and God's deliverance of the people from bondage. But more than simply a reminder of a historical event, the Jewish observation of Passover celebrates the continuing relationship between God and the people and God's continual saving acts in the lives of the Jewish people. Passover is thus a celebration of God's past actions (the Exodus), God's present actions in the life of the community, and toward God's future saving actions (sending a Messiah).

The Last Supper

(3–5 minutes)

Supplies

Bibles

Optional: Communion cup and plate as visual reminders

Read Luke 22:14-20.

The Bread

What does yeast (leavening) do when added to bread? *(It causes it to rise.)*

Leavening is sometimes symbolic of sin.

How can sin be like yeast added to bread dough? *(It spreads when we let it get started. It becomes a bigger and bigger part of your life.)*

The unleavened bread of the Passover is a reminder of God's grace and forgiveness of our sins.

Eucharist is another name for Holy Communion. It comes from the Greek word "eukharistia," meaning "thanksgiving."

The bread that Jesus used when he "broke the bread" is called the "afikomen matzah." The name means "I came" and is symbolic of the Messiah. Just as it was baked without leaven, Jesus was without sin. Just as it was broken by him, he was broken and died for us.

The Cup of Thanksgiving

When Christ said "Drink from it, all of you. This is my blood of the covenant, which is poured out for many for the forgiveness of sin," he was referring to the Passover lamb. Jesus is our Passover Lamb. Because he shed his blood on the cross, God will "pass over" our sin.

When Jesus and the disciples gathered to celebrate the Passover, he reinterpreted the original meanings of the meal. He compared the breaking of the unleavened bread to his body, which would be broken to nourish the people. He compared his blood, which would soon be shed on the cross, to the blood of the Passover lamb, which served as a sign of God's covenant with the Israelites. Jesus' blood became a sign of a new covenant between God and humanity.

Holy Communion

(10–20 minutes)

Supplies

Bibles, hymnals or books of worship, paper and pencils

The sacrament of Holy Communion is an "outward and visible sign of an inward and spiritual grace." The elements of the Lord's Supper are the bread and wine, symbolizing the body and blood of Jesus. These represent God's love and care for us.

Read Luke 24:13-35 (The Emmaus Meal).

As the two travelers sat to eat with the risen Lord, they recognized him in the breaking of the bread. Many people feel that, as did the travelers, Holy Communion provides a personal time of fellowship with Jesus.

Read John 21:1-19 (The Galilee Meal).

Here, the risen Lord appeared to Peter and some disciples on the Sea of Galilee. During the meal, the Lord led Peter to affirm his love and gave Peter the task of "feeding the sheep." At Communion, people can experience what Peter did: forgiveness, reconciliation, new hope, and mission.

Pass out copies of the ritual for Holy Communion. (Check your hymnal or book of worship.) The Communion ritual usually includes five parts:

1. **Invitation:** The pastor invites those who want to turn away from their sins and follow Jesus to take Communion.

2. **Confession:** Our confession helps our hearts be ready.

3. **Words of Assurance:** The Words of Assurance give us confidence that God forgives our sins. The Words of Assurance are verses in the Bible.

4. **The Great Thanksgiving:** This is when God is thanked for sending Jesus. During this time, the pastor asks God to bless the bread and cup so that when we take them we will remember.

5. **Words of Institution:** These are the words that the pastor says when Communion is given to you, reminding us what Jesus said to the disciples at the Last Supper.

Assign different parts of the Communion ritual to different youth (or groups). Have them review what is written in the ritual, and rewrite their parts in their own words.

Discuss: What does Communion mean to you?

Pray Aloud Together

Explain this type of prayer:

Tongsung Kido means "pray aloud" in Korean. Usually the congregation is given a specific theme for the prayer. Then, everyone prays aloud their individual prayers all at the same time. The voices of the other youth will not bother you if you simply concentrate on your own prayer.

Give a moment or two to center around the theme of Jesus' sacrifice for us. Begin praying at the same time.

† † † NOTE † † †

If you plan to do the Agape Feast (pages 73–74),

1. Use the parts written for the service of Communion during your Feast;

2. Explain to the youth that the Agape Feast was the forerunner to our modern-day worship service.

(2–3 minutes)

Program 6

AT THE CROSSROADS:
The Untouchables

Lenten Link

Jesus surprised his disciples by washing their feet. In doing so, he showed them how his followers are to live.

Focus

To demonstrate to youth the radical nature of Jesus' call to service to all, even those whom society calls untouchable.

Practice of Faith

Footwashing Service (pages 75–76)

Scripture

John 13:1-17

(5 minutes)

Holy Thursday

Invite the youth to recall what they know about Thursday of Holy Week and the Passover.

> On **Thursday of Holy Week,** Jesus gathered the disciples together in the upper room in order to celebrate the Passover. During this feast, Jesus and the disciples were remembering the slavery of the Israelites in Egypt and their release from bondage following the Passover.
>
> When God established the **Passover** in the Old Testament (Exodus 12), the Israelites were commanded to sacrifice a lamb without blemish and mark the doorways of their homes with the blood of the lamb. This way, the Angel of Death (in the 10th plague) would "pass over" the houses of the followers of God and spare the lives of the first born. The use of blood in the Passover was symbolic of the deliverance from sin, in addition to the deliverance of the Israelites from slavery.
>
> It was at the Passover feast that the final or **Last Supper of Jesus** with the disciples took place. We celebrate it now as Holy Communion. Another event, the **washing of the disciples' feet,** also happened at this time.

Jesus and the Untouchables

Read Matthew 8:1-3.

Untouchables. Throughout his ministry Jesus continually reached out to serve and heal persons whom society considered untouchable. There was an unwritten code, or caste system, that determined a person's social relationships and religious standings. Caste, what level you were on, was an important concern to the Jews of that time. Tax collectors, sinners, and Gentiles belonged to a caste that others did not associate with.

Lepers were among the lowest of the low. Leprosy was a terrible disease. Not only were persons with leprosy physically ill, but they were also considered ceremonially unclean. (See Leviticus 13:45-46.) Under the Old Testament law, those who were unclean were required to live apart from the rest of the community.

LEPER DEMONSTRATION

Bring the Leper in front of the group. Have the person remove his or her shoes and socks and put on the old clothes over his or her own clothes.

"Because they were isolated, lepers had no occupation. They were not afforded simple pleasures such as bathing."

Rub dirt on arms, face, and feet of the Leper; mess up his or her hair.

"That would be hard enough by itself, but leprosy is an awful disease. "

As you speak, make "sores" on arms, face, and feet by getting glue mixture on the toothpick and touching it to the skin area. Be sure that the sores are large enough that they are visible to the youth.

"It starts out with reddish sores that appear on the body, usually the arms, legs, and face. As the disease progresses, it affects areas of the body such as the hands and feet."

The Leper makes his or her hands into claws and curls up feet as much as possible.

"As the disease progresses, the sores begin to discharge. "

Use tweezers to grab clumps of the egg mixture and place them near the sores of the Leper. Be dramatic while applying the slimy, brown egg clumps.

"Lepers were outcasts in Jesus' time. They were excluded from the Temple area. Because of this, society viewed them not only as separated from community life but also separated from God. But Jesus often healed persons with leprosy."

Have the Leper take a seat.

Supplies

A good-humored volunteer to play a leper; old clothes large enough to fit over "the leper's" clothes (Clothes should be as dirty and ragged as you can get them.); white glue mixed with non-toxic tempera paint to the color of a reddish sore; whole egg mixed with a small amount of brown tempera paint; pair of tweezers; toothpick; dark dirt (such as potting soil)

(10—15 minutes)

Supplies

Large towel, pitcher of water, and basin

Read John 13:4-15.

"Following the Passover meal, Jesus gathered his disciples together and laid aside his outer garments and placed a towel around his waist."

Wrap a towel around your waist or drape it over your arm.

"He went to his disciples and with a basin of water. Jesus began to wash the dust and grime of the Jerusalem streets off of their sandaled feet."

Pour water from the pitcher into the basin.

"In this one act of submission, Jesus rocked the disciples' world. In the Hebrew culture, it was customary for the meal's host to provide a basin of water to allow their guests a chance to wash their own feet as they arrived at the house. In some cases he would have a slave do it. Others would not even require a slave to perform this task because it was seen as degrading and beneath the duties of a common household servant.

"What Jesus did by washing the disciples' feet was to put himself below the lowest of the low. That is why Peter objected. For Jesus, the footwashing had more significance than simply washing off the road dust."

Read John 13:8.

"After he washed all of his disciples' feet, Jesus directed them to continue to wash one another's feet."

Read John 13:14-15.

Go to the Leper, kneel down in front of him or her, and wash his or her feet.

Ask: By lowering himself to the status below household servant when he washed the disciples' feet, what was Jesus telling us? (*We need an attitude of service and love as we go out into the world. We need to touch the untouchable.*)

(5—15 minutes)

Today's Untouchables

Ask the youth to think of a modern-day example of someone who follows Jesus' teaching. Here is one:

In India, the culture contains a caste system similar to that in Jesus' time. This system is a moral system where a person is defined by descent, marriage, and/or occupation. Once a person is defined within a caste, it is impossible to switch to a different level. Contacts between the castes are limited, and the dirtiest work is left to persons in the lower castes. Marriages can only occur within the same caste. The untouchables in

India do not belong to any of the 3,000 castes. They are truly untouchable, the lowest of the lowly.

Mother Teresa of Calcutta has given us a modern example of Jesus' "footwashing attitude" with her work in India. In 1948 she began to minister to the sick and dying on the streets. This was a major action, because she and her missioners reached out to the people who were the untouchables among the Hindu culture of India.

Discuss as a group the following:

† Who are today's "untouchables" in our society? in your lives?

† What actions would be as "world changing" for us as the footwashing was for the disciples?

† Who are the untouchables in your lives? Is it someone who goes to your school or is it someone who lives down the street?

† What could you, as a group or as individuals, do to serve them in the attitude of the footwashing?

W°W♪D?

Give each youth a "WWJD?" (What Would Jesus Do?) bracelet.

"When you encounter persons whom our peers or our society says are untouchable, ask yourself, 'What would Jesus do?' Wear this bracelet as a reminder to be more like Jesus in your everyday life."

† † † NOTE † † †

Think of other persons whom you, and perhaps your youth, know who exemplify the servant attitude. They are often right in your own local church.

(2–4 minutes)

Supplies

"WWJD?" bracelets for each participant (available at Christian bookstores)

Optional: Print *WWJD?* on slips of paper or small pieces of card stock. Ask the youth to slip them into their wallets or backpacks.

Program 7

THE 'END' OF THE JOURNEY:
The Crucifixion

Lenten Link

We've sanitized, gilded, and glorified the cross. But death by crucifixion was unspeakable agony, which Jesus suffered for us all.

Focus

To challenge youth to deeper awareness and appreciation of the sacrifice of Jesus Christ upon the cross.

Practice of Faith

The Way of the Cross (pages 77–81)
or **Making a Palm Bouquet** (pages 70–72)

Scripture

1 Peter 2:22-25

† † † NOTE † † †

Note: This session will deal graphically with the agony Jesus suffered for us. It may not be appropriate for all youth. You may choose to delete parts; use your discretion.

(5–8 minutes)

Supplies

Bibles; copies of the handout "Jesus' Suffering and Death" (page 52)

Process for this Session

Give each youth a copy of the handout "Jesus' Suffering and Death" (page 52). Assign the various Scriptures to different youth. Have them locate their passages and mark their place in their Bibles to be ready to read them at the appropriate time.

Have everyone look up and mark **1 Peter 2:22-25** to read together later.

As you work through the session, have the youth read their particular passage. Make a list on the board of what happened to Jesus in each case. For example, write *In the garden* and *Sweated blood*; write *Hearing before Annas* and *Struck him in the face* beside it. Do this for all of the verses.

For most youth, the cross is a piece of nice jewelry; the Crucifixion, a sanitized death by a "superhero." The purpose of this session is to impress upon youth the suffering Christ endured as a sacrifice for *their* salvation.

"He bore our sins on his body on the cross, so that free from sins,
we might live for righteousness" (1 Peter 2:24a).

Jesus in the Garden

(4–6 minutes)

"Imagine for a minute that God gave us the ability to see into the future. With that gift you knew that when you left today, you would be in an automobile accident, would suffer, and finally die. How would you be feeling right now?"

"Because Christ was God, he knew what was going to happen to him. But because he was also man, he must have felt exactly as you would have while looking into your future."

Read Luke 22:41-44.

Sweating blood. Jesus was obviously agonizing when he prayed in the Garden. It is believed that here Christ experienced a medical condition known as "hematidrosis." Hematidrosis occurs when someone is under great stress. The usual response is to faint. When one does not faint, the blood pressure rises so high that blood vessels break and results in the mingling of blood and sweat from the forehead.

Supplies
Bible

Jesus Is Arrested and Tried

(10–14 minutes)

Read Luke 22:47-53.

The crowd coming to arrest Jesus were sent by the chief priests, elders, and teachers of the law. Included with the Jewish officials were soldiers.

Read John 18:12-14, 19-23.

Annas was the former high priest and was probably regarded by many to still be the high priest.

Read Mark 14:53-65 and Mark 15:1.

Caiaphas was the ruling high priest. The **Sanhedrin** was the high court of the Jews and included three kinds of members: the chief priests, elders, and teachers of the law. The high priest was the presiding officer. Under Roman rule, the Sanhedrin was given a great deal of authority, but they could not impose capital punishment.

Read Mark 15:2-5.

Pilate was the Roman governor of Judea. **Herod** was the king.

Read Luke 23:6-12.

Jesus was **ridiculed and mocked.**

Read Mark 15:6-15.

Flogging was not a simple thing. In the time of Christ, Roman society indulged themselves in all forms of cruelty. One thing they found great

Supplies
Bible, leather belt, small piece of thorn branch for each youth (or weave the branches into a "crown"); a large nail for each youth

pleasure in was inflicting pain on others. Crucifixion was designed in every detail to cause as much pain and torture as possible as the person died.

Soldiers prepared condemned men for the cross by scourging or flogging with a whip called the **"cat-o-nine-tails."** This whip was made of several strips of leather. Embedded near the ends of the strips of leather were pieces of broken bone, lead, or rocks with sharp edges. As the person was flogged, these sharp edges would tear into the skin and rip it off. The condemned received 39 lashes with this whip. The aim of the flogging was to remove all the skin from the back of the condemned without killing the person. This was done to intensify the pain and torture of crucifixion. Many people did not survive the flogging.

Have youth close their eyes. Hit a leather belt against a table or wall 39 times.

Read Matthew 27:27-30.

"Jesus was stripped and a **scarlet robe** put on him. What do you know about his back?" (*The flogging would have left his back with open wounds.*)

Hand each youth a twig with thorns or a "crown" made of woven thorn branches.

"Think about what it would be like to have this made into a **crown** and forced on your head. "

Read John 19:16b-17.

Review from the board the list of things that Jesus had endured up to this point.

The Crucifixion

(10–15 minutes)

Supplies
Bible; a large nail for each youth

Read Luke 23:26.

Draw on the board as you explain the following:

The **cross** didn't actually look like our cross symbols of today. Victims usually did not carry an entire cross. The upright part of the cross was permanently mounted in the ground. What the condemned carried was the heavy crossbeam. Due to Jesus' weakened condition, he was unable to carry the heavy crossbeam himself.

Read Luke 23:32-33.

Details of the Crucifixion are not given in the Bible, but history provides us with what being crucified was actually like. The person was laid on the ground with the cross bar above his head. The arms were pulled out and upward, and a nail driven through the top of the wrist.

Hand each youth a large nail.

Through experimentation and the study of anatomy, the Romans had discovered the **medial nerve**, located just above the wrist joint and the center of the foot. The weight of the body caused the nail to press against this nerve, shooting terrible pain throughout the body.

The victim was then lifted off the ground with one man on each side of the crossbar, lifting the suspended person on two nails. The crossbar was then dropped into the upright beam.

The legs were jacked up, with one ankle on top of the other. The reason the legs were jacked up was so the victim was able to breath. The only way to exhale was to lift with his arms and push up with his legs to hold himself up for a few seconds to allow the air to escape (remember Christ's back had no skin and he is pushing up against rough wood).

Hanging on the cross caused the bones, heart, and other internal organs to move out of their normal place.

Read Mark 15:24.

The solders **cast lots** (gambled) for Jesus' clothes. He hung nearly naked on the cross.

Read Luke 23:44-46.

Think quietly for a few moments about **Jesus' last words.** Repeat them over and over to yourself.

Read John 19:31-32.

Usually victims suffered on the cross for three to four days. Their **legs** were then broken, preventing them from being able to lift themselves up in order to breath. They then died quickly of suffocation.

Read John 19:33-37.

There are some who believe that the flow of **water and blood** from Jesus' wound is evidence that he died from a broken heart. Some people think of it as a symbol for the sacraments of baptism (water) and Communion (blood).

Making It Personal

(3—4 minutes)

Have everyone read **1 Peter 2:22-25.**

Ask: Why would Jesus do this? What do you gain from Jesus' sacrifice?

Optional: Distribute Cross in My Pocket crosses and cards.

Close with a prayer thanking Christ for his death so that we may live.

Supplies

Bibles

Optional: Cross in My Pocket® cards and crosses for each youth (available at most Christian bookstores for about 50 cents each)

Jesus' SUFFERING & DEATH

Luke 22:41-44 Jesus in the Garden

Luke 22:47-53 Jesus Is Arrested

JEWISH TRIAL

John 18:12-14, 19-23 Preliminary Hearing Before Annas

Mark 14:53-65 Trial Before Caiaphas and the Sanhedrin

Mark 15:1 Final Action of the Council

ROMAN TRIAL

Mark 15:2-5 Trial Before Pilate

Luke 23:6-12 Trial Before Herod Antipas

Mark 15:6-15 Trial Before Pilate Continue

Matthew 27:27-30 Jesus Wears His Crov

John 19:16b-17 Jesus Carries His Cross

Luke 23:26 Simon of Cyrene

Luke 23:32-33 The Criminals

Mark 15:24 Gambling for Jesus' Clothes

Luke 23:44-46 Death of Jesus

John 19:31-32 Breaking the Legs of the Crucified

John 19:33-37 Jesus' Side Pierced

1 Peter 2:22-25 He Bore Our Sins

DESTINATION EASTER!
The Great Commission

Lenten Link

Christ is alive! What good news! Death is not the final word. As the risen Jesus walked and talked with various people after the Resurrection, he commissioned them tell the good news to others.

Focus

To help youth share the message of Jesus Christ with their friends.

Practice of Faith

The Way of the Cross (pages 77–80) **or Youth Reaching Youth** (page 11)

Scripture

Matthew 28:16-20

Christ Is Truly Risen!

(10 minutes)

In the early centuries, Christians greeted one another on Easter with words meaning, "Christ is truly risen," to which the reply was, "Thanks be to God."

Use this greeting with the youth after explaining its origin.

The center of the Christian faith is in the Resurrection. Without the Resurrection, there would be no Christians. Read the story of the risen Christ's appearances. Assign different youth to different passages:

John 20:1-9	At the empty tomb
John 20:11-18	To Mary Magdalene at the tomb
Luke 24:13-32	To two travelers on the road to Emmaus
John 20:19-25	To ten disciples in the upper room
John 20:26-31	To eleven disciples in the upper room
John 21:1-23	To seven disciples on the Sea of Galilee
Matthew 28:16-20	To the disciples on the mountain in Galilee

Supplies
Bibles

Without the Resurrection, there would be no Christians.

(20 minutes)

The Great Commission

Supplies

Bibles; copies of "The Jesus Road" handout (page 55)

"The last Scripture read is called "The Great Commission." As followers of Christ, we are all to share the gift of grace and the story of salvation with others. But often times, we're not sure how to do that."

"The first thing is to understand how someone becomes a Christian. Becoming a Christian is to accept Jesus Christ as your savior and to invite him into your heart. When you do this, it is called 'conversion' (turning around) or 'making a commitment to discipleship.' Other terms you may have heard are 'being saved' or being 'born again.' The Bible tells of different types of experiences people have when they decide to follow Jesus."

Read Acts 9:1-19. Saul had a **dramatic experience** when he was on his way to Damascus. Many people will respond to Christ this way—suddenly and very emotionally.

Read Luke 19:1-9. Zacchaeus' conversion was different. He was curious and sought out Jesus. He then **made a decision** to become a follower.

Read 2 Timothy 3:14-15. Then there was Timothy. He could never refer to any one moment when he was converted. Surrounded by the example and nurture of others, he **grew in faith.** As Paul wrote, it was "from childhood."

Ask if youth can relate to any of these Bible persons. Invite them to talk about their own experience. (It would be good to tell your story too.)

Distribute "The Jesus Road" handout.

"In leading someone to Christ, some Native Americans use the imagery of walking on 'The Jesus Road.' It is a good way to explain the message of salvation to someone and to invite him or her to join you on that journey."

Assign the listed Scriptures to different youth. Read the handout, having the various youth read the Scriptures and also the explanations from the sheet.

In small groups or pairs, have them practice telling the story and inviting another person to accept the gift of Christ Jesus' great love.

† † † NOTE † † †

Be sensitive to the fact that there may be youth in your group who have not yet received Christ. If need be, provide an opportunity at the end of the session for these youth to respond.

(10 minutes)

Thanks Be to God!

"The Council of Nicaea in A.D. 325 prescribed that during Easter time all Christians should pray standing, never on bended knees. It is a way to symbolize that we are risen with Christ."

Have youth stand. Shout together:

"CHRIST IS TRULY RISEN! THANKS BE TO GOD!"

End with prayer, focusing on thanksgiving and asking for courage to share the message with others.

THE Jesus Road

When the Great Spirit created the world, he divided it into two great seasons, the warm and the cold. The warm season brings life and light. The grass springs up and the birds sing. There are new life and growth, joy and gladness.

The cold season brings death and darkness. The grass dies, the trees are bare, the fruits are gone, the animals become weak and poor—even the very water turns hard. There is no joy, no growth, no gladness.

The Jesus Road will lead you to summer where you will find life, light, and warmth. You'll have flowers and fruit, abundant life and growth. If you follow any other road, it will lead you to winter. You'll have no growth, no light, no warmth.

1 John 4:16 . . . tells us that . . . God is like the summer sunshine, bright and warm.

Romans 3:23 and Romans 6:23 . . . tells us that . . . No one is perfect. Because of our wrong doings (called sin), we are separated from God. Because of sin, everyone deserves to walk in the darkness of winter.

John 3:16 . . . tells us that . . . God wants us to experience the joy of summer. So Jesus, God's only Son, paid the penalty for our sins by dying on the cross. When he did that, he became the road from winter to summer.

Ephesians 2:8-9 . . . tells us that . . . People follow many paths, trying many things, searching for the warmth of summer. Some even try to buy road maps with things such as good deeds. But it is only by faith that we are able to walk down that road.

Revelation 3:20 . . . tells us that . . . Christ stands, knocking at the door to our hearts. All we have to do is to invite him in. He will come to be with us.

In order to experience all that summer has to offer, you need only admit that you too are a sinner and that you are sorry for all that you have done that has separated you from God. You accept that Jesus Christ gave his life for you, that he paid the price for sin (death) and can bring you back into right relationship with God. Invite him into your heart. When you do that, God will send the Holy Spirit to warm your life and guide you down the Jesus Road.

I'd like for you to experience life on the Jesus Road. Let us pray together.

ASH WEDNESDAY
Service

The following worship service was written especially for youth. Their participation in this experience will reinforce what they've gained from the Ash Wednesday study (pages 14–19).

If your church holds a congregational Ash Wednesday service, encourage your youth to attend. You may want to review the material below with them in advance so they will have a better understanding of the experience.

A good time to hold the service is before school on Ash Wednesday. Once youth have had this experience, they will be eager to tell others about it. Going to school with ashes on their foreheads will evoke questions from their friends. The ashes provide a great witnessing tool for them.

Before the youth arrive: Set up the worship area. Light the large candle.

BEFORE THE SERVICE, OUTSIDE THE WORSHIP AREA

Review the background information on Ash Wednesday (pages 14–17).

Provide a burlap bracelet to those participants who did not make one during the Ash Wednesday study. Tell them that the bracelets represent sackcloth.

Review terms your youth may not be familiar with:

> **Sin:** Actions, attitudes, or words that separate us from God and others.
>
> **Repent:** To admit that we are sinners and that we are sorry for what we have done, said, or thought that has been sinful.
>
> **Grace:** Because of God's grace (unearned favor) we are forgiven and given new life.

Distribute cards and pencils. Instruct participants to write on the card a particular sin or hurtful characteristic they have. Tell them no one will be reading their cards. When they have finished, collect the pencils; but have the youth keep their cards with them.

Instruct the youth to remove their shoes and socks.

Have everyone join hands and form a circle. Begin singing "Sanctuary." The worship leader leads the youth into the sanctuary or worship area, single file, still holding hands. The group faces the altar or worship area. The leader takes his or her place facing the youth. Continue singing "Sanctuary" until everyone is in place.

Supplies

A small amount of dried palms. If not available from last year's Palm Sunday service, check with a florist; purchase ahead to allow them to dry out.

Fireproof container or grate for burnings cards and palms

Large candle and a small candle

Small container for mixing ashes and water; scoop or spoon, towel

Card and pencil for each participant

A burlap bracelet for participants who did not make one during the Ash Wednesday study. As an alternative, braid three pieces of jute and then tie them on the participants' wrist.

Words to "Sanctuary" (or the recording from *Youth! Praise 2*)

The song "Grace," from Wes King's CD *A Room Full of Stories*

The Service of Worship

O God,
maker of every thing and judge of all that you have made,
from the dust of the earth you have formed us
   and from the dust of death you would raise us up.
By the redemptive power of the cross,
   create in us clean hearts
   and put within us a new spirit,
that we may repent of our sins
   and lead lives worthy of your calling;
through Jesus Christ our Lord. Amen.

From The United Methodist Hymnal, page 353

† † † NOTE † † †

You may wish to invite different youth to read the opening prayer and the various Scripture passages in the service.

Leader:

"Ash Wednesday is the beginning of the Lenten season. The use of ashes on this first day of Lent is derived from several ancient customs. In the Old Testament, people put on sackcloth and ashes when they were sorrowful."

From the Book of Daniel, we read:

To show my sorrow, I went without eating and dressed in sackcloth and sat in ashes. I confessed my sins and earnestly prayed to the Lord my God: Our Lord, you are a great and fearsome God, and you faithfully keep your agreement with those who love and obey you. But we have sinned terribly by rebelling against you and rejecting your laws and teachings.

Daniel 9:3-5 (CEV)

"The early Christians also wore ashes on their body as a visible sign of sin and a public request for forgiveness. During that time, people who had committed serious public crime would approach the church shortly before Lent to accuse themselves.

"Barefoot, dressed in sackcloth, with their heads bowed, they stood outside the church. They entered the church, the church leader leading one of them by the hand, with the others following in single file, holding each other's hand. Before the altar, as each sinner approached, the church leader imposed the ashes on his forehead in the sign of the cross.

"As time went on, relatives and friends began to show their humility by joining them before the church and asking to be marked as sinners too. Finally, the number of the self-condemned grew so large that the administration of ashes was extended to the entire congregation as it is today."

"In this way the whole congregation was reminded of the mercy and forgiveness proclaimed in the gospel of Jesus Christ and the need to renew our faith.

"I invite you, therefore, to observe Lent as holy. Do this by self-examination and repentance; by prayer, fasting, and self-denial; and by reading and meditating on God's holy Word.

"To make a right beginning of repentance, and as a mark of our mortal nature, let us now kneel before our Creator and Redeemer."

Adapted from The United Methodist Book of Worship (pages 322–323)

Have the youth kneel at the altar. The worship leader should collect cards from the youth, instructing them to take a few moments for silent prayer.

"God, we humbly kneel before you, as our forefathers did, barefoot with sackcloth to show our true sorrow for our many sins. These sins are represented by these cards *(place cards on grate; light small candle from large candle and ignite cards)*, which we offer as a symbol of our need for forgiveness."

From the Book of Isaiah, we read

> I, the Lord, invite you to come and talk it over. Your sins are scarlet red, but they will be whiter than snow or wool.
>
> **Isaiah 1:18 (CEV)**

Hold up palms and begin to burn them.

"God, we burn these palms to represent the renewal we receive through your grace. We know because of the sacrifice of Christ, we are forgiven and given new life."

From the Book of Romans, we read

> For sin will have no dominion over you,
> since you are not under law but under grace.
>
> **Romans 6:14 (NRSV)**

"God, we thank you for your wonderful gift of grace."

Scoop out ashes and mix with water. Go to each participant, placing the sign of the cross on his or her forehead.

As the leader begins to mix the ashes, begin playing the song "Grace." When ashes have been administered to everyone and the song is finished, close with the blessing:

Go in peace
with the understanding of
God's tremendous love for you and
God's generous gift of grace. Amen.

PETER'S Walk

An Overview of This Devotional Experience

In this experience, the youth will be blindfolded and asked to hold on to a long rope to keep them together. Guides will lead them through six areas or rooms where they will hear "Peter" telling about a significant incident in his walk with Jesus. In each of the areas, the youth will also experience something related to Peter's walk that will engage their senses.

Preparation

† Choose an area in the church or at a retreat center where enough rooms can be set up prior to the experience.
† Gather the supplies and set up the various rooms.
† Meet with guides, readers, and singer prior to event so that they understand their roles.

Participants

Work with small groups of no more than 15 on a rope. If your group has more than 40 youth, consider preparing additional rooms so the various small groups do not encounter long delays waiting for others to finish. With the team of guides, work through the logistics of moving a large group through the rooms. This activity has not only been done with very small numbers of people but also with more than 250 participants at one time.

Before the Walk Begins

Tell the group: This experience will encourage you to use all of your five senses. It is to be an experience of trust, because each of you will be blindfolded. There will be guides to lead you around after your blindfolds are in place. It is not important that you know who the leaders are, but it is important that you trust them to lead you.

Please know that no one will do anything to hurt or embarrass you during this activity. I ask that you do not talk. Just listen, and feel, and smell, and taste, and experience for the next hour some of the feelings and experiences that the disciple Peter might have had as he walked with Jesus.

† *Instruct the youth to take off their shoes and socks and put on a blindfold.*
† *Move them into single-file lines of about 15 participants.*

Supplies

Blindfolds; ropes (long enough for about 15 people to hold onto at one time); guides; readers for Peter, Jairus' daughter; readers for Scripture and for the closing; flashlights if needed for readers and singer

† † † NOTE † † †

The event is more effective when rooms and hallways are dark or dimly lit.

† *Place their right hand on the rope and their left hand on the shoulder of the person in front of them.*
† *Put the front person's left hand on the shoulder of one of the guides.*
† *The second guide for the group should stay in the middle or toward the end of the line to watch for any obstacles or problems.*
† *When the group is ready to begin their walk, read Peter's introduction.*

READ AS PETER:

You don't know me. We've never formally met. You have read about my life, part of it, that is. You never read about me as a child growing up, but you've heard about my life from the point where I met Jesus for the first time.

Sometimes when people read about my life in the Bible, they make it sound kind of boring and ordinary; but it wasn't at all. It was fascinating, exciting, frustrating, perplexing, and even scary.

I had no idea when I met Jesus that my life would change so much—even my name changed! I had always been called Simon, but Jesus told me that I would be called Peter, the Rock.

Jesus didn't change only me. He changed everyone he met in some way. I wish that you could have met and known him as I did. He was so special. I have so many memories. Come with me now . . . back in time . . . and relive some of my memories with me.

† *The guides now lead the group to Room 1.*
† *Once the group arrives, have them sit down.*

Room 1

READ AS PETER:

Supplies
Bible, baskets, pieces of bread, pieces of cooked fish

Being a disciple made me feel so important. We used to have mobs of people following us everywhere. Some people just wanted a glimpse of Jesus. Others wanted to touch him. Some even wanted to be healed.

Take, for instance, one day when we were outside of a town and people had come out to hear Jesus preach and teach. He was even doing miracles that day. It was lunch time; but none of the people, except for one little boy, had brought food with them.

Jesus told us to feed the crowds with the little boy's five loaves and two fishes. We all thought that he was joking around, but he was really serious. I couldn't believe my eyes. He blessed the food, and we started passing it out to everyone there.

There was always more in our baskets. We even had leftovers to pick up! To this day it is really hard for me to believe that it happened. But I saw it. And I ate some of the bread and fish too!

☩ *Have someone else read **Mark 6:41-42.***
☩ *Have the guides feed the youth pieces of bread and fish from the baskets.*
☩ *Then, begin walking to Room 2.*
☩ *When the group arrives, they are to remain standing.*

Room 2

READ AS PETER:

When we had finally finished eating (all five thousand of us), Jesus told us disciples to get into the boat and head for Bethsaida. He said that he'd get everybody else started home and that he wanted some time alone to pray. I wondered, as we shoved off, how or when or where we were supposed to meet him; but I figured that he had probably told John. So I settled back in the boat to relax.

Most of us were exhausted after working in that crowd all day. But none of us could sleep. We were still discussing all the baskets full of leftovers! By sundown we were almost halfway across the lake.

Suddenly, a strong wind came up; it looked like a bad storm was on the way. Everyone grabbed the oars. We rowed hard, but we weren't getting very far.

We were straining at the oars, just trying to stay afloat, when we saw someone or something walking out on the water. We figured that it must be a ghost. We were terrified. But then we recognized Jesus' voice talking to us from out on the lake.

I couldn't believe it! First, he had fed all those people and now this! What a day this was turning out to be. And before I realized it, I heard myself yelling to Jesus, "Hey, if it's really you, let me walk on the water to you." Jesus yelled back, "Come on!"

By this time, I realized what I had said. I really didn't want to go out there, but I couldn't chicken out now. (After all, everybody was watching me. I had my reputation to consider.)

So I stepped out. It was the strangest sensation—not to sink down into the water. The wind had picked up again and the boat was drifting farther and farther away. I panicked. But just about the time my head was about to go under, I felt a strong hand reach down and pick me up.

All night long, all I could think of was Jesus. How amazing! Truly, he must be the Son of God. And I had walked on water with him. No one would ever believe me.

Supplies

Bible, water, masking tape, garbage sacks, and towels

† *One at a time, have participants walk barefoot across water poured on plastic garbage sacks that are taped to the floor.*
† *Place towels at the end of the line for the participants to wipe their feet on.*
† ***The key*** *to this experience to let the youth take one or two steps without anyone guiding them, and then strongly grab their hand and lead them across.*
† *After everyone has walked across the water, line up them and move them to Room 3.*
† *When the group arrives, have them sit down.*

Room 3

Supplies

A volunteer to read the part of Jairus' daughter

Optional: tape recording of a young girl reading the role

READ AS PETER:

It didn't seem like a day ever went by that Jesus wasn't called upon to heal someone of some illness. He would always go out of his way to help, even to help the unclean lepers. He wasn't like any of the other religious leaders I had known. He really cared about people, even children.

Take, for example, the time that Jairus' daughter was sick. Jairus had begged Jesus to heal his daughter. We were on the way to Jairus' home when a servant came to meet us. He told us not to waste our time traveling any farther, because the little girl had died.

Jesus ignored everything the servant was telling us. He just kept walking toward Jairus' house. When we arrived, we saw the funeral preparations going on. Jesus told everybody that the little girl wasn't dead; she was just sleeping. But how did he know? He hadn't even seen her yet!

READ AS JAIRUS' DAUGHTER:

For days and days, I had lain in my bed with a fever. Mommy and Daddy had tried so hard to make me well. I overheard them whispering in bed one night. Daddy said that he had heard about a man named Jesus, who healed people. Mommy asked him if he would go see if he could find that man. At least, I think that was what she said. She was crying so much that it was hard for me to understand her. Daddy said that he would start out first thing in the morning.

The next thing I remember is a strange man leaning over me and smiling. He gave me a great big hug, and then he told Mommy to fix me something to eat. I guess that Daddy had found the man who could make me well.

I do remember one strange thing about that day. The man told everybody in my house not to tell anybody about what they had seen. I wonder what he meant by that.

   † *Lead the group to Room 4.*
   † *When they arrive, have the youth remain standing.*

Room 4

READ AS PETER:

The time of the day that I liked best was after supper, sitting around the fire. Jesus would be with the crowds all day, but in the evenings there were just the thirteen of us.

We talked about what had happened that day. We told jokes and had such good times, and once in a while Jesus would tell stories. No matter what he said or how he said it, I always learned something new.

I remember one night in particular. Jesus had been kind of quiet; and as he stared into the fire, I could tell that he had something on his mind. Finally, he broke up our conversation with one question: "Who do people say that I am?"

That wasn't a particularly easy question to answer because it seemed that everyone we knew had a different opinion. But we told him what we'd heard people say. Finally, he asked, "Who do you say that I am?"

All of us just sat there. How could he ask us such a question? What kind of answer did he want? Finally, I blurted out, "You are the Christ, the Messiah, the Son of the Living God."

There! I had said it. I'd been thinking about it for a long time, but finally I had told him. I thought that some of the other disciples might laugh, but nobody did. And then Jesus . . . well, he told me that I was blessed and that I would be known as Peter, the Rock.

And then he said something even more strange. He told me that he would build his church upon me. What did *that* mean?

- † *Give each participant a rock to hold in his or her hand.*
- † *Lead the group to Room 5.*
- † *When they arrive, have the youth sit down in chairs.*
- † *Pour warm water into bowls.*

Notes

Supplies

A rock for each participant

You are the Christ!

Room 5

READ AS PETER:

It was almost time for the Passover Feast. I'd always liked Passover, and I was looking forward to spending it with Jesus. Jesus had sent John and me on into Jerusalem to begin preparations.

He had told us where to go, who we would find, and what to do. I had seen so many miracles, but here was another mysterious happening. I still could not understand how he knew to tell us all of that.

It was such a strange evening when Jesus and the rest of the disciples arrived. Judas seemed awfully fidgety, and Jesus was somber. Jesus got up

Supplies

Chairs, bowls, pitchers of warm water, towels, a Bible, a hammer and a board, someone to sing "Were You There When They Crucified My Lord?"

from the table, wrapped his cloak around his waist, and poured water into a basin. He turned with the basin of water and a towel in his hands to face us.

I couldn't help but blurt out, "Lord, you are *not* going to wash our feet!" This didn't make any sense. He had just ridden into Jerusalem a few days before on a donkey—just like the promised king. Everyone had been shouting, "Hosanna! Blessed is he who comes in the name of the Lord!" How could the King of Israel, our Messiah, even think about doing a servant's duty? No! He mustn't be our servant! He is our Messiah!

But Jesus said that he had to, that if I was to be a part of his Kingdom I had to let him do that. I remember him looking at me, waiting for me to give my consent. Finally, I said, "Well, if you must wash my feet, please do my head and hands as well." I felt so unworthy and unclean.

But Jesus said that wasn't necessary. I watched him as he washed my feet, his hands lovingly doing that lowly servant task. Why? Why did he have to do that?

> † *The guides now wash the participants' feet.*
> † *Have someone read* **John 13:36-38**.

READ AS PETER:

A cock never crows without my remembering that awful night when Jesus was arrested.

I guess that I have always bragged a little too much or thought that I was capable of doing more than I really could. But when Jesus told me that night in the upper room that I would deny him three times, I just couldn't believe it. After all of the things he had taught me, after all of the things we had been through, I could *never* deny him.

But I did.

I remember the cock crowing. Three times I said I didn't know him. I wonder if Jesus told me that just so I would know that he knew how really weak I still was. I tried so hard to be perfect, to be strong, to be the best disciple that Jesus would ever work with; but Jesus knew how stupid I felt sometimes. He knew how scared I was too.

Maybe his telling me that it would happen was his way of saying that he understood, that he would forgive me, and that he would want me to keep working for him.

The worst part of denying Jesus was never getting the chance to tell him how sorry I was. They crucified him the next day.

> † *Hammer the the board as if driving in three different nails.*
> † *Create lightning effects with lights; loudly slam a door.*
> † *Then, have a time of complete silence.*
> † *Have someone sing "Were You There When They Crucified My Lord?"*

READ AS PETER:

It was all over. All my dreams of the great Kingdom, all my purpose was gone. Jesus was dead. I had spent three years of my life with him, and I had failed him. He was gone. Our future together was gone.

✝ *Go to the room where you began or to a worship setting.*

Room 6

Supplies
Bible

FINAL READER:

But that's not the end of the story! After Jesus' resurrection, we read these words from the Gospel of John. This was now the third time that Jesus had appeared to the disciples after he was raised from the dead.

✝ *Read John 21:14-17.*

Peter had the chance to respond again to Jesus' love. We have that chance too! No matter how many times we feel that we have betrayed Christ, he is always giving us another chance, asking us, "Do you love me?"

✝ *Ask participants to remove their blindfolds.*
✝ *Invite them to a time of silent prayer at an altar or in their seats.*
✝ *Close with prayer.*

PROCESSING QUESTIONS

✝ How did you feel?
✝ What did this experience tell you about Peter's discipleship?
✝ What does it tell you about your discipleship?
✝ How are you like or unlike Peter?
✝ Peter's walk was a life-long journey of discipleship. We relived some of the most powerful moments of that journey. What have been one or two significant events of your journey so far?

Adapted from "Peter's Walk," by Joye Perry, *Youth Teacher & Counselor,* Summer 1986. © 1986 by Graded Press.

A LAETARE Sunday

Focus

To allow the youth (and the leaders) participating in the Lenten study an opportunity to experience joy in Christian fellowship.

Laetare Sunday (Latin for *rejoice*) occurred on the fourth Sunday in the Lenten season. The early church called it a day of joy within the mourning season. It was originally established to give those participating in the Lenten fast a time of relaxation and rest so that they could continue on with a refreshed heart and spirit.

The idea behind this experience is to provide your youth (and yourself) a break from the rigors (and the seriousness) of the study without breaking their Lenten commitments.

On the fourth Sunday or during Week 4 of the study, have a youth group fun night. This fun night can include your youth's favorite youth group games. See below for some of our favorites, including ones from *Mudpie Olympics—And 99 Other Nonedible Games* (Abingdon Press). Or use this night to have an upbeat praise worship time of singing with your youth. The idea is to simply have clean, wholesome fun with your youth.

SUGGESTION 1: Go Gooey

Here are some fun recipes your youth can really sink their hands into. There are several rewards or good consequences to this fun time:

† Do some of your youth babysit? Let them try out these play recipes on themselves. Then the next time they are looking for something other than a movie to keep the kids occupied, they'll have something new to try.

† Is your church near a homeless shelter or domestic violence shelter with a lot of preschool- and elementary-age children. Help your youth make a bunch of these fun recipes and provide individual gift bags for a boredom-busting surprise for those children.

† Is your church preschool in desperate need for some new play dough and bubbles? Here's an inexpensive refill that your youth can make as a gift.

Are you ready for fun?

Supplies

Refreshments: Make sure that you have a wide variety so that if some of your youth have given up soft drinks or junk food for Lent, they will have something to eat too.

Creativity: Think of fun, inexpensive ways your youth can enjoy being Christians together.

Fun, Boredom-Busting Recipes

Face Paint

2 teaspoons shortening
2½ teaspoons cornstarch
1 teaspoon all-purpose flour
3–4 drops glycerin soap
food coloring

Mix all ingredients together
and have fun.
Makes enough for one color
to use for one child.

Gooey Glop*

1 cup white glue
1 tablespoon tempera paint
1 cup water
1⅓ cup warm water
¼ cup laundry booster (like borax)

1. In one bowl, mix together the first three ingredients.
2. In a second bowl, mix together the last two ingredients.
3. Add the first mixture to the second mixture. The mixture
   will then get stretchy.
4. Remove the Glop from the bowl, leaving any extra water
   in the bowl. Store the Glop in a sealed container.

* Not suitable for children under first grade.

Big Bubbles

6 cups water
2 cups liquid detergent
¾ cup white corn syrup

1. Stir together all of the ingredients.
2. Let the mixture stand 4 hours.
3. For bubble wands, use pipe cleaners, twist ties, clothes hangers, fly swatters.
4. Refrigerate between uses, but let the bubble mixture come to room temperature before use.

Slarch*

½ cup white glue
¼ cup liquid starch
food coloring

1. Stir together all of the ingredients
   in a small disposable plastic
   container.
2. Knead the mixture on a paper-
   covered surface until it is
   smooth. (This takes a while.)
   If the Slarch is too sticky, add
   teaspoon of starch; if it is too
   stringy, add ½ teaspoon glue.
* Must be used the same day—
   it doesn't store well. It's great
   for squishing and pulling.

Scented Play Dough*

3½ cups flour
½ cup salt
2 packages powdered soft drink mix
3 tablespoons vegetable oil
2 cups boiling water
food coloring (optional)

1. Mix together the first three ingredients in a bowl.
2. Add the oil and water. Stir it with a spoon.
3. When the mixture is cool, knead it with your hands. Add
   flour as needed to obtain the right texture.
4. Add food coloring if a darker color is desired.
* Do not cut this recipe in half. Makes enough for 3 medium-
   size projects. Play dough is great to play with but doesn't
   dry well. The creations do not hold their color well when
   drying.

Lots of fun games of your choice. (When choosing games, make sure to check for any props you may need.)

† † † NOTE † † †

Modify the ideas to fit the dynamics of your group. Remember, the idea is to have fun, and to leave at the evening feeling refreshed and ready to head into the second half of the Lenten season.

SUGGESTION 2: Play Hard

Sardines

This is an indoor game of Hide and Seek with a twist. Before the game, you might want to set some basic ground rules for where the youth may not hide.

1. Choose someone to be It.
2. It is to hide while the group begins counting to 100 in a whisper, gradually increasing in volume. By the time they get to 100, they should be shouting.
3. At the count of 100, the group separates to search for It.
4. When a person finds It, he or she hides *with* It, keeping very quiet. Each person who finds It stays in the hiding place with It and any others who have already found It.
5. Eventually, there will be just one person searching, and the remainder of the group will be with It, packed into the hiding place like sardines.
6. The last one to find It (and the rest of the packed-in sardines) becomes the new It, and the game begins anew.

Knots

1. Have the group stand in a circle.
2. Each person is to reach across the circle and take the hand of two other persons. When all of the players are holding hands, they will be a human knot.
3. Players untie the knot by turning around and going under the connecting arches of arms.
4. No one should let go of anyone else's hand until the human knot is completely untied and everyone is standing in a circle again.

Shuffle Your Buns

1. Place enough chairs for each participant into one large circle. Have each person choose a chair. Select a person to be It, who will stand in the center of the circle, leaving one empty chair.
2. The object for It is to sit in an empty chair. However, it is the object of the other players to prevent the leader from sitting. Each player slides to the left whenever the chair beside him or her is empty. The entire group is shuffling in a clockwise direction in an attempt to keep the leader from sitting down.
3. If It manages to sit in the empty chair, the person sitting to the right of It becomes the new It and must then go to the center of the circle and try to sit in an empty chair.
4. For added confusion and excitement, introduce the element of change. Announce that the direction of the circle will shift whenever you blow a whistle.

The Mystery Gift

1. Wrap the biggest candy bar you can find in numerous layers of newspaper and lots and lots of tape. (Masking tape works best.) The idea is to have many layers of paper and tape so that the gift will be hard to open.
2. Have the youth sit in a circle with the gift, a large coat, a large pair of gloves, a hat, and a scarf in the center of the circle.
3. The youth will take turns passing and rolling a die (half of a pair of dice).
4. Whenever a player rolls a 6, he or she goes to the center of the circle, puts all of the clothing on, and then attempts to open the package.
5. While this action is going on, the players continue to pass and roll the die.
6. When someone else rolls a six, the player in the center must stop trying to unwrap the gift and must take off the clothing. The new player puts on the clothing as it is being taken off by the other player and then tries to open the gift.
7. The game continues until the gift is finally opened. The person who removes the final layer keeps the big candy bar.

Supplies

Candy bar, newsprint, and masking tape, gather one large coat, one large pair of gloves, a hat, a scarf, and one die

SUGGESTION 3: Get Creative

1. Use play dough (recipe on page 67), markers, crayons, paper, and any other creative media you have on hand.
2. Invite the youth create or draw something significant that has happened to them during the study up to this time.
3. Give awards for the goofiest, the most artistic, the most creative use of available materials: If you can think it, award it!

Supplies

Play dough, markers, crayons, lots of paper, other creative media

† † † NOTE † † †

Encourage all the adult leaders to jump in and have fun with the youth too. It's good to laugh with your youth.

SUGGESTION 4: Hang Out

Have Christian music videos playing, bring out the board games, and give the youth a chance to simply hang out in a Christian setting. You might even bring out the flavored coffees and teas if your youth enjoy that.

SUGGESTION 5: Turn on the Tournament

If you have table tennis, air hockey, or something similar, start a tournament. Give fun awards for the best sport, the winner, the one with the fewest points, the one who yells the loudest. The fun awards are endless!

SUGGESTION 6: Praise God

Close the evening with a time of praise worship. Ask your youth for their favorite songs and introduce some new ones. Encourage everyone sing out. Make a joyful noise!

Supplies

Lots of praise songs, both fast and slow, such as those found in the *Youth! Praise* recordings

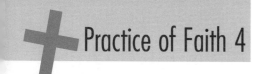

MAKING A
Palm Bouquet

Supplies

For *each* person——6-inch diameter (or larger) plastic foam ball; floral pins; Spanish moss (this is packaged very compactly and goes farther than you might think); ⅛- to ¼-inch ribbon (satin or shiny paper) in purple, royal blue, and gold; ¼- to 5/16-inch diameter dowel about 36 inches long or sticks about the same size; silk or fresh greens and flowers

Origins

On Palm Sunday most churches commemorate Christ's triumphal entry into Jerusalem with palm processions and the singing of "Hosanna." This is an ancient custom dating to the fourth century.

Throughout the world, this day is known by various names, depending on what plant is used in the procession. For example, it is called Flowering Sunday or Blossom Sunday in England, Willow Twig Sunday in Lithuania, and Willow Sunday in Poland.

In central Europe, the worshipers carry palm bouquets. A palm bouquet is a large cluster of plants fastened to the top of a wooden stick. It is interwoven with flowers and adorned with ribbons. Palm bouquets come in all sizes, from small ones to ones with sticks ten feet tall or more.

This is an opportunity for the youth to make a palm bouquet. They can carry the palm bouquets during the church's palm procession, interspersing the palm branch carriers and palm bouquet carriers.

Plants and Flowers

Any spring flowers and greens (either fresh or silk) would be appropriate for a palm bouquet.

If you are using fresh garden flowers or wildflowers, make the palm bouquets right before your worship service (perhaps during Sunday school time). Otherwise, the flowers may wilt.

If you wish to use fresh greens, a plant called Jade is available from almost any florist. It is inexpensive and looks like a palm leaf. Fresh flowers from a florist would be lovely, but they are generally expensive.

A number of plants and flowers besides the palm have traditional connections with the seasons of Lent and Easter. Give the youth the handout "Easter Legends of Flowers and Trees (page 71). You may also want to include the handout in your Palm Sunday worship bulletin for the whole congregation to enjoy.

EASTER LEGENDS ✝ HANDOUT
of Flowers and Trees

English Holly—English Holly is a glossy-leaved holly. This legend recounts how its white berry was turned to red from Christ's blood.

Willow—This legend tells how the willow once was a strong plant with thorns and was used to make Christ's crown of thorns. The tree wept and drooped at having caused Christ so much pain. This caused the sharp thorns to turn themselves into soft leaves that would never cause suffering again.

Lily-of-the-Valley—The legend is that the plant sprung up from the tears of Mary, the mother of Jesus, as she wept at the foot of the cross.

Larkspur—Jesus walked often in the Garden of Gethsemane. According to legend, there was a time when Jesus did not come to the garden; and all of his little animal friends missed him, particularly a little rabbit who waited day and night for his return. Early on the third day, Jesus came; and as he walked, he gave the little rabbit a loving smile. Later, when Jesus' friends came to the garden to pray, they found a path of flowers, the larkspur. To this day, one may see in the center of each blossom an image of the little rabbit who waited three days and three nights to greet the risen Lord.

Veronica—Legend tells that on his way to Calvary, Jesus passed the home of a humble woman. As he passed her, he sank under the weight of the heavy cross he was carrying. She gave him her veil to wipe his brow. From the sweat that fell to the ground sprouted a blue-flowering plant in which a tiny image appeared in each dainty bloom. The flower was called Veronica after the women who befriended Jesus.

Apple Tree Blossoms—The Tree of Knowledge in Genesis is traditionally referred to as an apple tree. An Easter legend tells that this Tree of Adam was eventually used to produce the wood for Jesus' cross.

Oak—A Christian legend from Greece tells us that all the forest trees, except the oak, revolted at the idea of being selected to provide the cross. Jesus pardoned the oak tree because it accepted death with him. The legend further tells that it was under the shade of a oak that Jesus appeared to the disciples after his Resurrection. Since that time, the tree has lifted its branches to heaven as if praying.

Dogwood—An American legend tells that at the time of the Crucifixion the Dogwood tree was the size of an oak and other forest trees. Since it was firm and strong, it was selected as the wood for the cross. To be used this way upset the tree; and Jesus, nailed upon it, sensed this. He said to the tree: "Because of your regret and pity for my suffering, never again shall the Dogwood tree grow large enough to be used as a cross. Henceforth, it shall be slender, bent, and twisted; and its blossoms shall be in the form of a cross— two long and two short petals. In the center of the outer edge of each petal, there will be nail prints, brown with rust and stained with red; and in the center of the flower will be a crown of thorns. All who see it will remember."

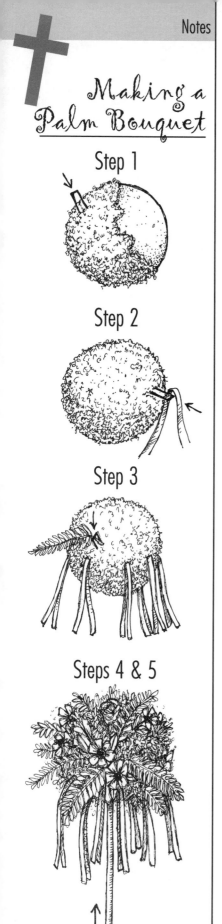

Making a Palm Bouquet

Step 1

Step 2

Step 3

Steps 4 & 5

Art by Barbara Upchurch

Ribbon Colors

When distributing supplies to the youth, take the opportunity to explain the liturgical colors used in worship services.

Ask: "Did you ever notice that different colors are used in the church at different times of the year?"

Say: "In the church, we use different colors for stoles and other vestments, altar cloths and other paraments, and church decorations during different seasons of the church year. These different colors are referred to as the 'liturgical (worship ritual) colors.'

"The use of these colors is based on ecumenical (the Christian church as a whole) tradition. This tradition originated with the desire to express the mood of the various celebrations. Different colors have different meanings.

"We have selected three colors—purple, royal blue, and gold—to use on our palm bouquets."

Tell the youth the following:

> **Purple** represents penitence and royalty. It is used during the seasons of preparation: Lent and Advent.
>
> **Gold** and **white** are joyous and festive colors used during both Christmas and Easter.
>
> **Royal blue** is sometimes used during Advent; it is the color of hope.

Making a Palm Bouquet

Step 1: Cover a plasticfoam ball with moss, using floral pins. (Moss is packaged very compactly; separate and fluff it first.)

Step 2: Cut various lengths of ribbon and pin them to the ball. Visualize where the bottom will be, and remember that the ribbons will be hanging down.

Step 3: Secure the ends of the greenery to the ball with floral pins. Only the ends should be fastened all the way around the ball so that they will stick out from the ball instead of being tight against it. Keep in mind where the bottom of the ball is.

Step 4: Secure the ends of the flowers in the same way as you did with the greens. Be sure that the blooms are not hidden by the greenery. Keep in mind where the bottom of the ball is.

Step 5: Push the stick into the bottom of the ball. Carry your Palm Bouquet by the stick.

THE AGAPE *Feast*

Sharing a Meal Together

In Bible times, sitting down at a table to share a meal with someone meant that you accepted that person. Mealtime was a religious experience. The table of fellowship enjoyed daily by the first Christian believers gradually gave way to a weekly meal referred to later as the "Agape Feast." (*Agape* means brotherly love.) Over time, these feasts grew into our weekly worship services.

Typically, the feast was held in the home of a wealthier member, who had the space to accommodate several families. The elder may have presided over the service, assisted by the deacons.

Rather than sitting in a chair around a table for a meal, Romans reclined on a mat or padded dining couch around a low table. They would prop themselves up on their elbows. People usually ate their food with their fingers and dunked their bread in their soups. Fruits, cheeses, and fish were commonly served. People washed their hands frequently during the meal.

First, Believe

In order to participate in this common meal, the person first had to be a member of the church. To be a member of the church, the candidate had to make a profession of belief in Jesus as Lord and in the Resurrection.

> So you will be saved, if you honestly say "Jesus is Lord," and if you believe with all your heart that God raised him from the dead. God will accept you and save you, if you truly believe this and tell it to others.
> **Romans 10:9-10 (CEV)**

> Don't you know that all who share in Christ Jesus by being baptized also share in his death? When we were baptized, we died and were buried with Christ. We were baptized, so that we would live a new life, as Christ was raised to life by the glory of God the Father.
> **Romans 6:3-4 (CEV)**

Most of what we know about these celebrations comes from Paul. His letters include instructions on how the meals were to be conducted, words of advice against eating and drinking too much, and guidelines as to the general tone of the occasion.

Supplies:

Food (see page 11 for suggestions), bread and juice for Holy Communion

Optional: Low tables

The Feast

Entering

On entering the room, have youth greet one another with a "Holy Kiss" (a kiss on the cheek). Boys kiss boys and girls kiss girls. (Yes! It was really done like that!) This practice was common in the early church. It is based on Paul's instructions:

> Greet one another with a holy kiss.
> **2 Corinthians 12:12**

Seat the youth. Following the seating, the elder (pastor) should lead the youth in prayer. Follow the opening prayer with the Lord's Prayer. It is commonly understood that the believers also recited the Lord's Prayer at the Agape Feast.

At the beginning of each meal, under the direction of the elder, all would partake of Holy Communion. Have the pastor lead the youth in Communion. Use the words written in Program 5 (pages 40–43).

Everyone would then say with great enthusiasm, "Maranatha!" (*Maranatha* means "Our Lord, come!") Explain the custom, and invite the youth to show their own enthusiasm.

Eating

Then everyone would eat. After the supper came the educational part of the program. This included the stories and teachings of Jesus. The guests would have listened to letters from their important leaders, such as Paul, which included practical advice for their own conduct. They also discussed problems. With the elder acting as moderator, everyone was able to participate in the discussion.

Take this opportunity for youth to ask the pastor questions they may have concerning their faith. You may want to have ready a starter question or two. The pastor could also talk about his or her favorite Scripture or story in the Bible.

Ending

The service probably closed with singing a hymn and repeating together a benediction the believers had learned, such as the following:

> May God bless you with his love, and may the Holy Spirit join all your hearts together.
> **2 Corinthians 13:13b**

A FOOTWASHING
Service

Before the Youth Arrive

† Set up the worship area. Place the basin, the pitcher of water, and the towel on a table with a large lighted candle.
† Lower the lights in the room.
† Place the chairs in a semi-circle, with the table as the main focus.
† Have the CD or tapes of the instrumental music cued up and ready to play as soon as the foot washing begins.

As the Youth Arrive

† Have an adult leader meet the youth at the door, and bring them into the worship setting.
† Have them sit in the chairs within the worship circle.
† Have your music leader playing quiet praise songs in order to set the mood for the event (quiet and worshipful).

The Worship Begins

Once all of the youth arrive, greet them and explain to them that they are about to experience a foot washing service, much like Jesus and the disciples took part in after the Passover meal. Lead them in the singing of a chorus of "Sanctuary" and "From the Rising of the Sun."

Read John 13:1-20.

Ask all of the youth present to remove their shoes and socks.

Explain to the youth what it meant in the disciples' lives that Jesus washed their feet. In the Hebrew culture, not even the lowest household servant was required to wash the muck and grime off of a traveler's feet. By washing their feet, Jesus went from royalty who came into Jerusalem on Palm Sunday, to servant.

Fill the basin with the water from the pitcher. Place the basin and towel on the floor in the middle of the circle.

† † † NOTE † † †

This worship experience closes with a service project. Decide beforehand what project your youth could participate in immediately following the footwashing service.

Supplies

A basin or bowl for the water

A pitcher of water

A towel to dry off their feet

Enough chairs for everyone to sit in.

A copy of the words to "Sanctuary" (*Youth! Praise 2*)

A copy of the words to "From the Rising of the Sun"

Soft instrumental music to play during the actual foot washing.

Plans for an immediate service project, and adequate transportation to this site.

Optional: WWJD? bracelets for those who did not receive them during Program 6 (available at Christian bookstores)

† † † *NOTE* † † †

Yes, some youth will giggle and squirm at the idea of someone touching their feet. This is a good chance to expose them to the uncomfortable and world-changing feelings the disciples experienced when Jesus washed their feet.

As the music begins, the leader kneels down of the floor and washes everyone's feet. Another option is to have the leader wash the first youth's feet, and then the youth wash one another's feet around the circle.

As the last person finishes with the foot washing, close this portion with another chorus of "Sanctuary."

The Service Begins

Re-read John 13:12-17, where Jesus explains how the disciples were to go out and serve those around them.

Explain to the youth that now they will have an opportunity to serve others. Have them put their shoes and socks back on, and lead them out to the waiting vehicles. Encourage them to remain silent and reflective on what they have just experienced. (Have your drivers turn their radios and car phones off before starting the engine. Encourage them also to stay quiet.)

Travel to your chosen mission project, such as a soup kitchen, and allow the youth to experience serving as Jesus did.

Reflection

Gather the youth together at the close of the service project. Ask them some of the following questions:

† What did it feel like to have your feet washed? Was it embarrassing or uncomfortable?
† What were you thinking about as your feet were being washed?
† What was it like to participate in this service project?
† If you have participated in other projects, did it seem different after you had experienced the foot washing service?
† What are some other ways you can live out Jesus' example of service within your community, school, work, and life?

Reminder

As a closing, you may choose to give those present a "WWJD?" (What Would Jesus Do?) bracelet. Encourage them to wear the bracelet as a reminder of Jesus' servant heart in every situation, regardless of what society dictated.

THE WAY OF The Cross

The Way (Stations) of the Cross originated in the time of the Crusades. Pilgrims would follow in prayer and meditation the route of Christ's way to Calvary. They would stop along the way at different stations, each one representing a different moment of Christ's final journey.

Today, methods used in presenting the Way of the Cross are only limited by one's imagination. One factor remains the same, however. That is, there is a definite stopping point along the way for each Scripture that is used in the story.

Traditional stations of the cross contain some stations that are non-biblical. The following version includes only stations with a biblical basis. In addition, the number of stations (the original has 14) has been condensed to ten so it can be used by all sizes of youth groups.

Station 1:	Luke 22:39-44	Jesus prays alone.
Station 2:	Luke 22:47-53	Jesus is arrested.
Station 3:	Mark 14:61-64	Sanhedrin tries Jesus.
Station 4:	Luke 23:1-24	Pilate tries and sentences Jesus.
Station 5:	Matthew 27:26-30	Jesus wears a crown.
Station 6:	Matthew 27:33-43	Jesus carries his cross.
Station 7:	Luke 23:39-43	Criminals speak to Jesus.
Station 8:	John 26:26-27	Jesus speaks to Mary and John.
Station 9:	Luke 23:44-45	Jesus dies on the cross.
Station 10:	John 19:38-42	Jesus is laid in the tomb.

Focus on the Process

The focus of this activity should be the studying of the Scriptures and the working together as a group—not the outcome. Allow the youth the opportunity to create the stations themselves. The suggestions below will encourage them to be creative within the limits of your situation. How they do the stations will also be dependent upon the size of the youth group, the location, the time, and the resources that are available.

There is no set way to do a station. Draw upon your own creativity.

Location

† If you have large grounds at your church, you may want to consider setting up some or all of your locations outside.
† If you have long halls and enough doorways, you could set up a station in each doorway or room.
† If you have a small church, you can have all of the stations in the sanctuary or fellowship hall.

Suggestions for the stations

† If you have costumes and props readily available, each station could include a frozen motion scene.
† If you have lots of doorways, place a white sheet in front of each door and a spotlight (work light) behind actors as they act out the Scripture. Since only their shadows are seen, props could be made of cardboard and costumes could be bathrobes and sheets.
† If you live in a large city, your stations could be at different locations that could be representative of Jesus' ministries and teachings such as a homeless shelter, a jail, a soup kitchen, and so forth.
† If you are limited to one room, get a roll of 4-foot-wide paper and have the youth draw the different scenes of the Way.
† Create worship banners for each station.

Some additional ideas

† Allow the youth to develop the Way of the Cross for your congregation and invite them to attend.
† Light the "way" with luminaries. These can be made with lunch bags, with a few inches of sand in the bottom, and a votive candle.
† Keep the lights out and give participants a candle to carry to light the way.
† Have group leaders carry a large cross as they lead people to the various stations.

What to do at each station

† Read the Scripture that pertains to that particular station.
† Play or sing a meditative song.
† Have youth write a meditation for each station to be read there.
† Have youth explain the station in their own words.

Planning the program

† Provide the youth with background information on the Way of the Cross.
† Provide Scripture sheets for the youth.
† Designate a youth chairperson for the project.
† Allow the youth chairperson to take over the meeting and coordinate the program. (A planning worksheet to guide the group is provided on pages 79–81.)
† Make it clear that all of the youth need to be involved.

THE WAY OF
The Cross

Station 1:	Luke 22:39-44	Jesus prays alone.
Station 2:	Luke 22:47-53	Jesus is arrested.
Station 3:	Mark 14:61-64	Sanhedrin tries Jesus.
Station 4:	Luke 23:1-4	Pilate tries and sentences Jesus.
Station 5:	Matthew 27:26-30	Jesus wears a crown.
Station 6:	Matthew 27:33-43	Jesus carries his cross.
Station 7:	Luke 23:39-43	Criminals speak to Jesus.
Station 8:	John 26:26-27	Jesus speaks to Mary and John.
Station 9:	Luke 23-44-45	Jesus dies on the cross.
Station 10:	John 19:38-42	Jesus is laid in the tomb.

Planning Sheet

Who will we be doing this for?
❏ Other youth groups
❏ Our parents
❏ Our congregation
❏ The whole state

When are we going to do it?   Date _____ Time _____

Be sure to check your church calendar!   Calendar Checker _____

How will we let them know?   Advertising Executive _____
❏ Church newsletter
❏ Church bulletin
❏ Phone calls   Callers _____
❏ Personal invitation
❏ Massive TV and radio campaign

Where are we going to do it?
❏ Outside
❏ In church rooms
❏ In town location   Place _____
❏ Sanctuary
❏ Fellowship hall
❏ Church roof

The Way of the Cross

What WILL EACH STATION LOOK LIKE?
What WILL BE DONE?
BY WHOM?

Station 1 _____

Station Manager _____

❏ Scripture Reading _____

❏ Music _____

❏ Singing_____

❏ Meditations_____

❏ Dancing _____

❏ Pantomime or freeze _____

❏ Other _____

Station 3 _____

Station Manager _____

❏ Scripture Reading _____

❏ Music _____

❏ Singing_____

❏ Meditations_____

❏ Dancing _____

❏ Pantomime or freeze _____

❏ Other _____

Station 2 _____

Station Manager _____

❏ Scripture Reading _____

❏ Music _____

❏ Singing_____

❏ Meditations_____

❏ Dancing _____

❏ Pantomime or freeze _____

❏ Other _____

Station 4 _____

Station Manager _____

❏ Scripture Reading _____

❏ Music _____

❏ Singing_____

❏ Meditations_____

❏ Dancing _____

❏ Pantomime or freeze _____

❏ Other _____

Station 5 _____

Station Manager _____

❑ Scripture Reading _____

❑ Music _____

❑ Singing_____

❑ Meditations_____

❑ Dancing _____

❑ Pantomime or freeze _____

❑ Other _____

Station 6 _____

Station Manager _____

❑ Scripture Reading _____

❑ Music _____

❑ Singing_____

❑ Meditations_____

❑ Dancing _____

❑ Pantomime or freeze _____

❑ Other _____

Station 7 _____

Station Manager _____

❑ Scripture Reading _____

❑ Music _____

❑ Singing_____

❑ Meditations_____

❑ Dancing _____

❑ Pantomime or freeze _____

❑ Other _____

Station 8 _____

Station Manager _____

❑ Scripture Reading _____

❑ Music _____

❑ Singing_____

❑ Meditations_____

❑ Dancing _____

❑ Pantomime or freeze _____

❑ Other _____

Station 9 _____

Station Manager _____

❑ Scripture Reading _____

❑ Music _____

❑ Singing_____

❑ Meditations_____

❑ Dancing _____

❑ Pantomime or freeze _____

❑ Other _____

Station 10 _____

Station Manager _____

❑ Scripture Reading _____

❑ Music _____

❑ Singing_____

❑ Meditations_____

❑ Dancing _____

❑ Pantomime or freeze _____

❑ Other _____

Along the Path

A COMPANION

FOR THE JOURNEY

This journal will help you study, pray, and record your thoughts as you journey through the season of Lent and Easter.

Each week has one Scripture. Each week has three steps. You may do the steps once during the week or make notes more often throughout the week.

No one will look at your journal, so write whatever is on your heart and in your mind. Happy journaling!

PREPARING FOR THE

Journey

Scripture Reference: Daniel 9:3 and 2 Corinthians 5:17

1. What did I learn this week that I can apply to my Christian walk?

2. What do I need to change in order to apply this to my life?

3. What is my plan to implement this action?

YOUR TRAVELING COMPANION: John

Scripture Reference: 1 John 1:1–2:17 and 2 Corinthians 5:17

1. What did I learn this week that I can apply to my Christian walk?

2. What do I need to change in order to apply this to my life?

3. What is my plan to implement this action?

BEGINNING THE *Journey*

Scripture Reference: Luke 19:28-38

1. What did I learn this week that I can apply to my Christian walk?

2. What do I need to change in order to apply this to my life?

3. What is my plan to implement this action?

ARRIVING AT
the City

Scripture Reference: Mark 11:11, 15-17

1. What did I learn this week that I can apply to my Christian walk?

2. What do I need to change in order to apply this to my life?

3. What is my plan to implement this action?

AT THE CROSSROADS 1:
Last Supper

Scripture Reference: John 13:1-38

1. **What did I learn this week that I can apply to my Christian walk?**

2. **What do I need to change in order to apply this to my life?**

3. **What is my plan to implement this action?**

AT THE CROSSROADS 2:

Untouchables

Scripture Reference: Luke 22:19-20

1. What did I learn this week that I can apply to my Christian walk?

2. What do I need to change in order to apply this to my life?

3. What is my plan to implement this action?

THE "END" OF THE Journey

Scripture Reference: Luke 22:44-45

1. What did I learn this week that I can apply to my Christian walk?

2. What do I need to change in order to apply this to my life?

3. What is my plan to implement this action?

A NEW Beginning

Scripture Reference: 1 Peter 2:22-25

1. What did I learn this week that I can apply to my Christian walk?

2. What do I need to change in order to apply this to my life?

3. What is my plan to implement this action?

NOT THE STUFF IN *Your Belly Button!*

Lent is coming!

Get Ready!

Is it time? Are we there yet? Is it time to start? Endless questions. Have you ever bugged the fire out of your parents asking stuff like this on long road trips? I mean, you knew that you were miles from your destination, but the anticipation was building up and if you didn't ask the questions you were going to explode! (Kind of like the shaken soft drink theory—if you don't open the top, the can or bottle might explode from the pressure.)

Now, think back to how you felt the night before school started in September. Did you get that butterfly-almost-nauseous feeling as you waited for classes to start the next day. One year I got so excited (and nervous) about starting classes the next day, that I checked at least 10 times to make sure that I had set my alarm clock. (Needless to say I didn't get much sleep.)

In the next few weeks, you are going to go on a journey. This journey will take you through the forty-day period known as the Lenten season. Along the way, you will encounter Christ as he prepares for the events of Holy Week and Easter.

There will be lots of stops along the way as you encounter some of the events and even the emotions that Christ and the disciples felt.

Hope to see you soon!

Notes From Your *Fearless* Leader

✝ Crazy Lenten Facts

Did you know that the word *Lent* comes from the Old English word *lencten,* which refers to the lengthening of days and the coming of spring.

COMING EVENTS

READ Ahead

What do the following Scriptures have in common?

Genesis 7:4
Exodus 16:35
Exodus 24:18
Matthew 4:2
Acts 1:3

The Mailing Address Goes Here

The Return Mailing Address Goes Here

Not Just The Stuff in Your Belly Button!

NOT THE STUFF IN
Your Belly Button!

Lent begins on Wednesday.

Ash Wednesday

Have you ever watched a fire burning? In the beginning (especially if you set it) it starts out small, just the size of the match head. But the fire doesn't stay small. It grows until it consumes everything burnable in its path. The fire destroys everything, regardless of individual worth.

Sometimes fires are started on purpose. In the mid-west, prairie fires are started in the fall to clear away the dead brush, which accumulates through the normal growing seasons. These fires are controlled and only burn within a certain area. From a distance, it looks like everything is being destroyed, without a purpose.

Yet, once the dead brush burned out, new plants and flowers begin to flourish, and by the time spring and summer rolls around, the prairie looks better than ever. Sometimes we have to burn out some of the "dead brush" in our lives. And while it looks like everything is destroyed, ultimately new life begins to bloom and we become a new person.

This week we are going to experience some of the cleansing power of fire, no we aren't going to burn the church down, but we are going use ashes to discover how new life can come from something dead. Come on and check this out. It's really cool.

Notes From Your *Fearless* Leader

Crazy Lenten Facts

Did you know that pretzels were once known as "little arms" because if you turn them upside down, they look like little arms crossed in prayer?

COMING EVENTS

READ Ahead

Sackcloth and ashes, what do those have to do with Lent? Read Daniel 9:3 and 2 Corinthians 5:17 for more details.

The Mailing Address Goes Here

The Return Mailing Address Goes Here

Not Just The Stuff In Your Belly Button!

NOT THE STUFF IN
Your Belly Button!

2nd week of Lent

John and Peter

Do you ever feel as if you are insignificant? as if whatever you decide won't really change the way things are going? Sometimes when I read the newspaper, I get really depressed. It seems like there is all this bad stuff going on, and regardless of what I do, it's going to continue.

Sometimes I just want to yell, "Stop the ride! I've had enough! It's just not worth it. I'm ready to leave now, God!" It seems like, regardless of what I do or say, bad things are just going to continue.

I wonder if Peter and John, and the rest of the disciples, wanted to get off the "ride" after Jesus was crucified. This man had changed their whole world, and now he was dead. And then when he did come back, instead of staying with them, to keep the early church alive, Jesus went to be in heaven, leaving the disciples to carry on without him.

In the face of death threats and other traumas, Peter and John were left to carry the Christian message out into the world. Pretty challenging for a bunch of former fishermen, huh? And yet, Christ used those guys, and a few others, to reach out to the entire world. So the next time you feel like what you are doing won't really matter, just remember how Christ used just a few ordinary disciples to reach millions!

Notes From Your Fearless Leader

✝ Crazy Lenten Facts

Which disciple was most like a teenager? Come this week and find out!

COMING EVENTS

READ Ahead

Which disciple is referred to as the one whom Jesus loved? Check out the fourth Gospel for the answers! (It's in there six times!)

The
Mailing
Address
Goes
Here

The Return
Mailing Address Goes
Here

Not the Stuff in Your Belly Button!

NOT THE STUFF IN *Your Belly Button!*

3rd week of Lent

Palm Sunday

The crowd went wild! USA, USA, USA! The skaters for the 1992 Winter Olympics team had been picked. What an incredible thing to watch as Nancy Kerrigan and Tonya Harding skated together as a team. Look out world, here come the Americans!

Then tragedy struck (literally) as a lone figure clubbed Nancy over the knee, to knock her out of contention for an Olympic metal. The world was riveted to the TV set, watching and waiting for the culprit or culprits to be caught.

I'm not sure who was shocked more to learn that the person behind the assault was Nancy's team partner Tonya. It seemed as if one minute the two were skating together as friends, and now, they were part of an international incident.

I wonder if this is similar to how Jesus might have felt riding into Jerusalem on Palm Sunday. I mean, he must have known that the people, who would cheer "Hosanna," on Sunday, would be the same people to turn around on Friday to yell, "Crucify him! Crucify him!"

It was as if Jesus were knowingly setting himself up for the ultimate betrayal and rejection; and yet he still went on, into Jerusalem.

Sometimes it's hard to forgive those people in our life who betray and hurt us, especially if they are friends.

Jesus showed the absolute form of forgiveness. He paid with his life.

Notes From Your *Fearless* Leader

✝ Crazy Lenten Facts

What do Florida and Easter have in common? Come this week and you'll see!

READ Ahead

Check out what Luke 19:28-38 says about Palm Sunday. Why did the people wave the palm branches?

Not the Stuff in Your Belly Button!

NOT THE STUFF IN
Your Belly Button!

4th week of Lent

Trouble in the Temple

Do you ever get so angry, that steam comes out of your ears? Or do you go and sit in a corner and sulk when things just don't go your way?

Anger is an emotion that occurs in everyone. How you deal with anger is based a lot on your personality. Each of us deals with things that grate on our nerves differently.

Lots of people tried to make Jesus angry; they wanted to see what he would do when he was really riled up. One thing that set him apart from the world is how he dealt with the anger.

Instead of blowing up at the slightest provocation, Jesus thought about his actions, and then came up with a strategy to deal with the issue. He also examined his motives, and always acted out of love.

How do you deal with anger? Are you a Hot Head? a Clam? An Avenger? a Martyr? Come to this week's study to see where you rank on the anger scale. You may be surprised to find out the solutions that the Bible has to help you deal with all of the irritations in life.

Notes From Your Fearless Leader

Crazy Lenten Facts

What do moneychangers, animal sellers, and a marketplace have in common with God's Temple? Come this week and check out the answer.

COMING EVENTS

READ Ahead

Check out Mark 11:11 and 11:15-17 to see what happened when Jesus entered into the Temple.

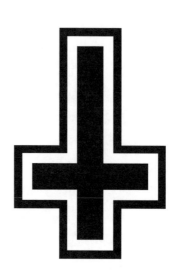

The
Mailing
Address
Goes
Here

The Return
Mailing Address Goes
Here

Not the Stuff in Your Belly Button!

NOT THE STUFF IN
Your Belly Button!

Surprise Supper

Have you ever gone to visit a friend and had something totally unexpected happen? I mean, you think that you are going for a simple meal or visit, and instead you walk into a surprise party.

The disciples had something unexpected happen to them during the Passover meal. They assumed when they gathered at the upper room, that they were going to celebrate the Feast of Unleavened Bread, just as they did every year. Instead, Jesus started talking about the New Covenant, and how the bread and wine represented something totally different—his body and blood.

The disciples didn't know what to think. Here was Jesus identifying himself with the bread and wine found at a common, everyday meal.

In this act, Jesus wanted to make sure the disciples remembered the primary message of the Last Supper every time they ate: that grace and forgiveness is found through Jesus.

This week we are going to look into some of the things that led up to Jesus' New Covenant and the Last Supper. So, come on in and check it out, it's going to be life changing.

Notes From Your *Fearless* Leader

✝ Crazy Lenten Facts

What do kissing and agape have to do with the Last Supper? Come this week and find out!

READ Ahead

Check out Luke 22:19-20 to get an idea about exactly what the Last Supper was.

The Mailing Address Goes Here

The Return Mailing Address Goes Here

Not the Stuff in Your Belly Button!

NOT THE STUFF IN *Your Belly Button!*

Footwashing Newsletter

Water plays an important role in our life. Did you know that 98 percent of your body is actually water? On a hot day a drink of water refreshes you after a long sweaty bike ride or basketball game. Water also brings new life to dying plants. Water is so vital, that without it, we would not exist.

Water plays a significant role in some of my favorite psalms. Many times the psalmist talks about the cleansing and purifying aspects of running water. Often the cleansing or fulfilling nature of water is compared to a deep longing for God.

OK, think about a time when you came home hot, sweaty, and dirty—You were so dirty and smelly that no one in your family would even acknowledge you. Think about how the water felt as it washed all of the dirt and muck away down the drain. Now think about how you felt and looked when you got out of the shower. I'll bet you felt like a totally different person.

Jesus used water to teach the disciples a lesson in cleansing the spirit as well as the body. Come this week to check out what they learned. You might be just as surprised as they were!

Notes From Your Fearless Leader

✝ Crazy Lenten Facts

What do smelly socks and water and Jesus have in common? The answer comes in this week's study.

COMING EVENTS

READ Ahead

This week, check out John 13:1-38 before you come.

Not Just The Stuff in Your Belly Button!

NOT THE STUFF IN
Your Belly Button!

Garden/Arrest/Crucifixion

One experience I had during Easter affected me so profoundly that I still remember it years later. It involved a mime drama that portrayed the events from the Last Supper through the Crucifixion. No words were used, but the facial expressions and movements conveyed the story vividly.

I was watching the drama just fine until it came time for the trials of Jesus. As the actors mimed kicking, hitting, and spitting on Jesus, I almost stood up and shouted "No! You can't do that! Don't hurt him!" I sat through the rest of the service numb as I watched Jesus "die" on the cross and get carried into the tomb.

Why would he go through so much pain and agony for me? Wasn't there any other way for Jesus to save the world without having to die?

The answer is no. Jesus had to die so that the common sinners (you and me) might live. Sometimes it's hard to understand everything surrounding Jesus' crucifixion. The Crucifixion definitely wasn't pretty. But it is crucial to our Christian faith. Without the Crucifixion and the Resurrection, Christianity wouldn't be the same.
This week we are going to explore what happened during Jesus' arrest, trials, and ultimately, the Crucifixion; so bring your questions.

Notes From Your *Fearless* Leader

✝ Crazy Lenten Facts

Did you know that Jesus suffered from a condition called Hematidrosis when he was in the garden? Come this week to find out just what this is!

READ Ahead

This week read Luke 22:44-45.

The Mailing Address Goes Here

The Return
Mailing Address Goes Here

Not Just The Stuff In Your Belly Button!

NOT THE STUFF IN
Your Belly Button!

No longer Lent

Easter

Wow! What a journey we've been on. We've experienced so many different things, everything from anticipation, joy, betrayal, forgiveness, anger, and death all within a forty-day period.

Now what do we do? I mean, what exactly does this Resurrection thing really mean? Does it have anything to do with me?

Yes, the journey is over. Christ has risen. But it's not the ending; instead it's the beginning. It's a chance for new life and a fresh start.

Now is your opportunity to grab hold of the promises that Christ offers through the Resurrection.

So where do we go from here? Throughout the world, Christians gather together each year to celebrate the new life found within the Resurrection. We are called Easter People. We rejoice in the promises that Jesus gave Christians through his death on the cross—and more important, through his Resurrection.

How can we (our youth group) become true Easter People? How can we share the good news given to us through the Easter message? Think about it. The answers will rock our world!

Notes From Your *Fearless* Leader

✝ Crazy Lenten Facts

Did you know that Easter has been known as the "Sunday of Joy"? It was once thought in Europe that the sun would dance for joy because of Christ's resurrection on Easter Sunday. People thought that if they got up early enough and went up into the hills, they would be able to see the sun leap about the clouds.

COMING EVENTS

READ Ahead

Read some of the Resurrection accounts in the Gospel. Check out Matthew 28:1-20 and John 20:1–21:25.

The
Mailing
Address
Goes
Here

The Return
Mailing Address Goes
Here

Not Just The Stuff in Your Belly Button!

DESTINATION Easter

Take a Walk With

Jesus

Peter

John

- - - - - - - - **Come along**

Giving Up Something for Lent?

Find out who has given up the most and why

See you there • • • • • • • • • • • • • •